Mak... as a **Radio** or **TV** Presenter

Making it as a Radio or TV Presenter

An Insider's Guide

Peter Baker

PIATKUS

First published in Great Britain in 1995 by
Judy Piatkus (Publishers) Ltd of
5 Windmill Street, London W1P 1HF

The moral right of the author
has been asserted

A catalogue record for this book is available
from the British Library

ISBN 0-7499-1452-1

Edited by Liz Hornby
Designed by Chris Warner

Data capture & manipulation by
Phoenix Photosetting, Chatham, Kent
Printed and bound in Great Britain by
Butler & Tanner Ltd, Frome, Somerset

CONTENTS

INTRODUCTION

Why do so many people want to become presenters? For fame? For the money? As an outlet for natural exhibitionism? Or simply because they want to be loved?

Ask yourself why you're prepared to:

- work crazy hours in all sorts of (usually unhealthy) locations?
- put on a happy and contented act even on days when you're neither happy nor contented?
- live constantly on the knife-edge of job security?
- have the risks of your private life being in the public eye?

Answer: Because you want to. And you'll *love* it.

The sad thing is that many people don't even bother to try to get into broadcasting as they feel it's a 'closed shop'. What is even sadder is that even more people go about it the wrong way. This book will explain the workings of the broadcasting world, and show you all the possible routes to your chosen career, with many tips and hints that I have collected from my years in the industry.

The unusual hours and variable working conditions may put people off, but the rewards can make up for everything. Good money plus the chance to perform in front of possibly millions of people can't be ignored. You also get to go where the public (the punters, as they are outrageously called in the media) *can't* go. You may be given press passes to royal visits, free tickets to shows, invitations to celebrity parties, the opportunity to visit behind the scenes at nuclear installations, crown courts or sausage-canning factories. In addition you may be sent free review copies of CDs, video releases and books. You will have the opportunity to interview celebrities, and you'll probably get recognised in the street.

Yes, of course, the competition for jobs is stiff. But don't let that put you off; everyone has to start somewhere and you could have just the right attributes to host a television or radio show.

Multi-skilled broadcasters

Many presenters today survive by being able to offer many different skills. What do you do, for example, when, as a freelance TV presenter, you come to the end of a series? Wait for the phone to ring? No, you badger for other kinds of associated work that you could do. Maybe you could do some commercial voice-overs, TV continuity announcing, comedy scriptwriting or presenting some radio shows. It keeps money coming in, and it keeps your 'face in the flow'.

Never forget my 'Broadcasting Law of Usefulness':

The more skills you can offer a TV or radio station, the more useful you will be to them.

It sounds obvious, but take this example: If you were a radio station boss in hard times and had to sack one of these presenters, both of whom had equal ratings, who would you dismiss:

■ The DJ who is just that. He comes in, does his show and goes home.

■ The DJ who not only presents a programme, but also pipes up with excellent promotional ideas in meetings. He has trained his voice to do station commercials, has learnt to drive the multi-track production studio, and knows how to programme the music computer.

A pretty easy choice. Throughout this book, I'll be suggesting ways in which you can hone your skills towards multi-skilled working.

Bi-media broadcasters

These are people equally at home in either radio or TV. Organisations like the BBC now actively encourage bi-media working practices and have set up joint radio / TV newsrooms and production areas. Moreover, in these uncertain times, as I mentioned above, the more skills anyone can offer, the better. I have been one of these animals for over eleven years now, and the variety can be stimulating and refreshing. On your radio show you can be working off-the-cuff, talking about all the burning issues of the day, then you might spend the afternoon at a TV station with a team working out a detailed documentary script which needs a lot of preparation before broadcasting.

I especially appreciate radio work when I'm booked to be 'just' a TV presenter. It can be frustrating to hang around a lot, keeping your lip zipped when another director is calling the shots, especially when you think you know better. A radio show is excellent therapy. You can say virtually what you like and you are in control.

If you become a radio presenter and then decide to 'go up' into television, don't burn your boats. Keep your hand in radio if time allows in your new TV contract. You will never regret it. Radio may not pay as well, but it can offer virtually continuous employment if your programmes continue to be popular, and can be a much more enjoyable medium to work in.

The basic requirements

So what qualities and/or qualifications are needed to be a broadcaster?

A VOICE   A must, of course, if you aim to major behind the microphone. If you feel that your voice is too thin or that you have a few bad habits, don't worry. In Chapter 13 I'll share with you some secrets about how to optimise your vocal capabilities.

INTELLIGENCE   Common sense and a knowledge of any subject you are dealing with will be essential. You can't be an expert in everything, but if you enjoy and keep up-to-date with contemporary music, you're halfway to a job in music radio; if you're an expert in politics and current affairs, you may be well placed to be a documentary reporter.

QUALIFICATIONS   All potential bosses like to see a string of certificates you have gained over the years, and in a way broadcasting is no different. Of course the number of top TV and radio presenters who are well qualified is balanced by the number who left school early and picked it all up along the way.

My advice is that if you have reached the stage in life at which you can take advantage of the educational system without blowing a good break.... do it. Unless you have a very good reason to leave school, stay on and then try for an appropriate college or university course. The benefits are obvious: you'll gain in maturity and worldly wisdom and those qualifications may prove to be essential job-hunting ammunition if broadcasting doesn't work out for you.

More on what kind of courses to choose later, and Factfile 1 gives details of specific training opportunities for broadcasters.

ENTHUSIASM What is it that keeps broadcasters working long and hard hours perfecting details on their programme? Is it pure enthusiasm, or are there a few elements of obsession and bullheaded stupidity in there as well? If you have the urge to learn, work hard and deal with an endless variety of changing problems, then you will make it in broadcasting.

EGO Seen as a bad thing in general society; however, presenters seem to need to have larger egos than other mere mortals in order to drive their careers. They are thrilled to see their names or pictures in magazines and thrive on the kicks of seeing their reports through the windows of TV rental shops.

Ego can get out of control, however, and I have known presenters who constantly look round in public to see who is looking at *them*. I have seen radio DJs walking through city streets with their headphones round their necks, or having themselves paged by friends in top hotel lobbies so they can rush to the telephone looking important. Sad, really, isn't it?

Chapters 14 and 15 give you hints on how to use your natural ego constructively and to your best advantage.

Check your skills

Here's a list of jobs. Scan down the list and see which jobs you genuinely feel you could attempt.

- Actor
- Barperson
- Bingo caller
- Circus performer
- Dancer
- Disco DJ
- Holiday courier
- Host in a holiday camp / theme park
- Musician
- Nurse / First-aider
- Photographic model
- Receptionist
- Scriptwriter

■ Shop assistant
■ Singer
■ Stand-up comedian
■ Teacher
■ Voice-over artist
■ Waiter / waitress

You will see some connection between the jobs listed above: every one of the occupations has some skill which is needed in the world of radio or TV presentation. For example, actors are trained to memorise scripts and to interpret them; photographic models have had to lose their inhibitions in front of a camera lens; scriptwriters have originality and creativity; nurses and first-aiders should be caring individuals who can relate to human beings; receptionists and shop assistants should be able to communicate well with the public; voice-over artists will have developed a great quality of voice and know how to handle a script, as well as having a good sense of timing; *all* of them (with the exception of the scriptwriter) need to be able to present a professional face and communicate positively with the public even when they're feeling miserable.

So you know you have what it takes. All you have to do now is prove it.

Note   A book on the broadcasting industry inevitably contains terms and jargon peculiar to broadcasting. I have aimed to explain these when they first appear in the text, and Factfile 4, *The A to Z of Broadcasting*, provides further enlightenment.

CHAPTER 1
THE UK BROADCASTING INDUSTRY

The BBC

*T*HE British Broadcasting Corporation, funded by public licence fees, runs two network television channels, **BBC 1** and **BBC 2**, and five network radio services broadcasting nationwide: **1 FM** which broadcasts pop and rock; **Radio 2** which aims entertainment programmes at an older audience; **Radio 3** which is the BBC's outlet for classical music; **Radio 4** which is the home of speech and current affairs; and **Radio 5 Live** which transmits rolling news and sport and is a little more populist than Radio 4.

Although its headquarters is in London, the BBC has three 'centres of excellence', in Birmingham, Bristol and Manchester, as well as forty-two local radio stations, and offices all over the UK. The Birmingham base (Pebble Mill) specialises in daytime and leisure, multicultural and drama television programmes. Bristol's strengths are natural history, documentaries and features, while Manchester is home to youth programmes, religion and sport.

Including Birmingham, Bristol and Manchester, there are thirteen main regional television newsrooms which produce bulletins and regional news programmes that at times opt out of the main output broadcast from London. These include the three centres in Wales (Cardiff), Scotland (Glasgow) and Northern Ireland (Belfast).

The BBC broadcasts radio outside the UK via the **World Service**, which has over 120 million listeners every week. This is funded direct from the government. **BBC World Service Television (WSTV)**, is self-funded by advertising, subscription and sponsorship and transmits across Europe, Africa, Canada and Asia by satellite.

Commercial television (terrestrial)

ITV is the umbrella title to describe a network of sixteen commercial broadcasters which cover the UK. The ITV Network Centre in London decides the shared programme schedule for all the ITV stations, providing a centralised programme commissioning system.

In recent years, many ITV companies have cut staff in order to become leaner and more competitive. One of the catalysts of this was the 1991 licence bid. Companies now have to pay an annual licence fee to the Treasury which ranges from **Central's** £2,000 to **Carlton's** £43 million. Read any of the recent union magazines such as BECTU's *Stage, Screen and Radio* and you'll hear of the continuing dissatisfaction of TV production staff with management's budget-cutting programmes. The argument is that if you cut budgets, quality suffers. Both GMTV and Carlton have been censured by the Independent Television Commission for poor standards in certain areas. The one gleam of hope in this apparent gloom is that ITV companies have to maintain the number of regional programmes made – traditionally the starting place for new TV presenters.

Channel 4 used to be funded by ITV companies, in return for selling its advertising time. Now, it is run as a public company and sells its own advertising. Most programmes are not made at Channel 4 itself, but bought in from independent producers. In Wales, the fourth channel is licensed to S4C (**Sianel Pedwar Cymru**), which has to broadcast around thirty hours of Welsh-language programmes each week.

The Independent Television Commission (ITC) regulates ITV as well as Channel 4, Teletext, and cable and satellite services based in the UK.

Satellite

The main satellite broadcasting to the UK is operated by **BSkyB**, based in Isleworth, Middlesex. Its multi-channel operation is funded by subscribers who pay to watch, and by advertising. Since most of the satellite channels show continuous movies or bought-in programmes, presenters and reporters will find most opportunities at BSkyB's **Sky News**, or one of the sport channels.

MTV Europe is housed in the old TV-AM building in London and is backed by the huge American Viacom operation. Presenters are employed to link the music videos; but the VJs, as they are called, have to know their music inside out. Featuring mainly rock and dance music, MTV also broadcasts bought-in music features and programmes.

Cable broadcasting

Cable offers the advantage of providing all four terrestrial TV channels and satellite television services without the need for an aerial or satellite dish. There are over sixty cable franchises covering a potential two million homes. Some cable stations have their own local programmes as well, offering opportunities to presenters.

The **Cable Television Association** will tell you who your local cable franchisee is and whether programmes are originated by the franchisee. The **Independent Television Commission** (ITC) also has a booklet with most cable companies listed. It's called *The Fact File*, and you can call them on 0171 255 3000.

Independent radio

Independent Local Radio (ILR) started in 1973 and today there are three national independent channels (Classic FM, Virgin 1215, and Talk Radio), and five regional ones, to complement the ever-growing list of local radio services. There are also temporary low-power radio stations called RSLs (Restricted Service Licences). They usually run for a month at a stretch; their duration is often tied in with a local event or festival. Over 600 RSLs have been put on the air so far. They provide a wonderful opportunity for newcomers to broadcast on or actually to run a radio station. The Radio Authority will tell you if a project is about to start in your area, or give you a fact pack if you want to set one up yourself.

The **Radio Authority** issues licences and regulates commercial radio by ensuring that they follow codes on programming, sponsorship, advertising, etc. The Radio Authority is also responsible for looking after cable and satellite radio services which are originated in the UK.

CLASSIC FM This station offers a twenty-four-hour diet of classical music and informed speech. A populist version of Radio 3, its audience has grown spectacularly since its launch in 1992.

VIRGIN 1215 Launched in April 1993, Virgin's output is aimed at a rock-music-loving audience. The AM waveband is prone to interference and the station is in low fidelity mono, but Virgin attracts an average of about three million listeners.

TALK RADIO Talk Radio, which was launched in February 1995 using BBC Radio 1's old medium wave transmitter network, reaches 96% of the UK population. It broadcasts speech programmes aimed at the 25–45 age group twenty-four hours a day. The brief for presenters and producers is to be upfront and irreverent.

REGIONAL RADIO There are five so-called 'superstations' which were launched in autumn 1994. The licences were awarded on condition that the output should 'broaden the range of audience choice', which was taken as being different in each region. Century Radio covers the North East with pop music and personality presenters; Galaxy Radio is the Severn Estuary's regional station offering dance music for younger listeners; Heart FM is based in the Midlands broadcasting soft adult contemporary music; JFM 100.4 covers the North West with a mix of jazz, blues and soul similar to that played by its mother station, JFM 102.2, in London; and Scot FM broadcasts speech and adult contemporary music to central Scotland.

INDEPENDENT LOCAL RADIO (ILR) The 144 ILR stations cover virtually the whole country, broadcasting music with a populist – some critics say 'bland' – approach. Many stations operate two services from one location, usually a 'Gold' service on AM which plays classic hits or 'oldies', with a more contemporary, younger feel on FM stereo.

OVERSEAS BROADCASTING The biggest radio station that doesn't come under the control of the Radio Authority is **Long Wave Radio Atlantic 252.** This transmits from County Meath, Eire, but has offices in London. It covers about 65% of the UK. Vienna's **Blue Danube Radio** is an English-speaking service which covers most of Austria. The station offers regular three-week-long contracts to presenters. A working knowledge of German would be an advantage in order to communicate with other staff. If working abroad appeals to you, the **Commonwealth Broadcasting Association** can give you a list of English-speaking TV and radio opportunities in places such as Hong Kong, Singapore, Australia, Zimbabwe, St Lucia, Malta and Sri Lanka.

If you speak a European language fluently, TV contacts across Europe can be sourced from the *European Television Directory*. For addresses of European radio and for TV stations further afield, the *World Radio and TV Handbook* lists virtually every station there is, including military services as remote as the **American Forces Antarctic Network!**

Other broadcasting opportunities

If weather presentation appeals to you, then it's worth knowing that virtually all the top on-air weather experts have qualifications in meteorology, and have been trained in presentation skills, not the other way round. The **Meteorological Office**'s personnel department will send you information on joining their organisation if you are genuinely interested in weather prediction. ITV's national weather is provided by **International Weather Productions**. The door is not totally closed if you haven't meteorological qualifications; some TV stations prefer to pick weather presenters who 'look right' and give them scripts provided by experts.

Traffic reporting inserts are sometimes provided to radio stations by outside companies. They employ presenters at many locations around the country. **AA Roadwatch** and **RAC Road Data** are service providers of travel news to broadcasters.

As you go through this book, you'll discover there are as many different ways in to the industry as there are people in it. Broadcasting opportunities can occur at any of the organisations I've mentioned, but you have to be realistic. If you are young and inexperienced, there's no point in angling to anchor *News at Ten* or to replace an established star on a gameshow. BBC and commercial local radio provides the best means of getting a foothold, not because standards are lower, but because there is a higher turnover of staff.

Non-broadcast opportunities

When you are looking for your first break, don't forget that there are TV and radio stations based around retail outlets. Asda, Texas, Topshop and larger HMV stores have a 'distributed' radio service. The Meadowhall shopping centre in Sheffield even has a TV service for shoppers. There are also producers whose programmes never get transmitted but who make corporate, publicity, and training videos, audio storytapes, or marketing cassettes. Standards in this industry can be as high as broadcast programmes and fees to presenters and voice-over artists can be excellent, too. Indeed, many of today's top names supplement their incomes very well by fronting non-broadcast videos or by chairing business conferences.

It would be impossible to list all the UK production companies in this book; I suggest you consult the *Broadcast Production Guide* or look up companies in the *Yellow Pages*, under these sections: Audio visual services; Film and video production services; Video services. Obviously, call each company first to see if they are in the market to use voice or presentation talent such as yours, and then mailshot using your CV and cassette just as you would to broadcasting operations.

Factfile 3, *The Contacts*, gives information to help you make contact with the organisations mentioned in this chapter, and addresses/phone numbers for the publications.

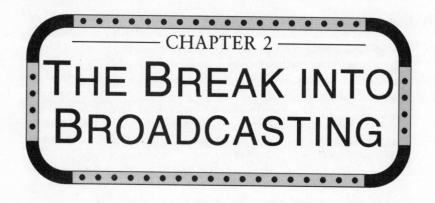

CHAPTER 2
THE BREAK INTO BROADCASTING

I HAVE WRITTEN THIS BOOK to give people the best possible chance to realise their ambitions in broadcasting, whether they already have a first step on the ladder or are still on the outside looking in. If you're reading this as an outsider to the industry, one question must be paramount in your mind:

How on earth do I get a break?

Broadcasting can seem to many like a completely closed and incestuous business, where 'who you know' is a more important factor than any talent you may possess. Let's look at the hard facts.

It is estimated that only 20% of production and 5% of presentation jobs are ever publicly advertised. Even when a job is advertised, you can be sure that a fair proportion of these advertisements are placed for reasons of legality or internal politics, and the successful candidate has already been chosen. Don't let this put you off, however. Terry Wogan had his first break by replying to an advert in a paper for an announcer's job for Radio Telefis Eireann. My own TV break came after I spotted an ad in the Creative and Media jobs pages in Monday's *Guardian*. A month or so after that fateful purchase in the newsagents, I was reading regional TV news bulletins for BBC West.

The *Guardian, Broadcast* magazine and *Stage and Television Today* are all useful publications to buy regularly or scan at the library. If you have a friend who can get you a copy of the BBC's weekly staff magazine, *Ariel*, take the opportunity, but be aware that most of the vacancies in it are for experienced internal candidates only.

A good way to acquire an overview of the system at the BBC and the sorts of jobs that are available to outsiders is to ask them for a copy of an information pack called 'The Way In'; it's available free of charge. Call up the corporation's Recruitment Services on 0181 752 5252.

Even if a job that might suit you down to the ground is not advertised at first in the press, you'll get to know the kinds of positions that are available, and the names and titles of the people in charge of operations.

Tip: Never throw any job adverts away. Even if they're past the 'reply-by' date, the information in them is invaluable background material if you manage to get an interview in the same department or programme office.

Job adverts are rarely aimed specifically at school leavers, but it is still important to get the 'lie of the land'. Only by understanding the kind of programmes being made will you see junior opportunities to apply for, like a runner's job on a new quiz series or manning phone-lines on a new radio station.

'Isn't it all a matter of luck?'

Being in the right place at the right time was how broadcaster Ned Sherrin got into broadcasting: 'I was walking down the Strand in London in 1955, and I literally bumped into someone I knew from Oxford who was now in TV. He asked me what I was doing. I replied that I was about to become a barrister. "We're starting commercial television tomorrow," he said. "Why don't you come and join us?" I was offered a TV producer's job the next day!'

Ned Sherrin may have been prevented from working at the Bar by that amazing bit of luck, but Clive Anderson spent fifteen years as a barrister before his lucky break. 'My leisure time was taken up by working as a TV studio audience warm-up man, and doing the odd bit of stand-up comedy. Not the most common hobby for a barrister, but there you are. I had a late-night phone call offering a job filling in on the radio programme *Cabaret Upstairs*, to be broadcast the next day! Of course, I accepted.' Regular radio and then TV work followed, and the legal profession was put on the back burner. Clive Anderson's advice for newcomers? 'Fifteen solid years as a barrister is essential!'

Angus Deayton had no real ambition to become a performer of any kind, apart from as a professional footballer. He had set his sights on a teaching career until his performing talent became evident in a university revue: 'One of the actors suddenly dropped out, and I was offered a part.' He then went on to write and perform the radio spoof programme *Radio Active*, which led him on to the successful TV and radio career he enjoys today.

Although previously established as a fashion model, Emma Forbes won her on-air break thanks to her knowledge of cookery. Contacts she made at the BBC secured her a cookery feature on *Going Live* where she demonstrated her enthusiasm for kids' cuisine in front of live TV cameras. This launched her into the *Talking Telephone Numbers* series and many other projects. She has also worked on *Hearts of Gold*, quite a few satellite programmes and has worked in the corporate TV sector.

'Don't you need to know someone?'

Not everyone was friends at university with a television producer. If you have no contacts at all in broadcasting, now is the time to start making them. This book is full of tips on how to seek out and impress the people you have to get to know, with a comprehensive Factfile on *Organisations* so you can ring up and start your own book of broadcasting contacts. Danny Baker's first contact book was filled with rock stars. After leaving school, he worked at a record shop in London which happened to be frequented by many of the top pop and rock artists of the time. This helped to fuel his enthusiasm for music, and he became one of the top writers for the *New Musical Express*. When he had 'friends in the business', and armed with an incredible memory for facts and information, along with his natural effervescent personality, he was perfectly placed for a move into broadcasting.

Starting at the bottom

Set your sights high but be prepared to start low. Even though there are more on-air opportunities than ever before, with an ever-expanding radio and satellite industry, competition for jobs is extremely high and only a fool would hang his or her future career on the sort of chance situation or lucky phone call which came the way of some of the presenters mentioned. Persistence, determination and professionalism are essential qualities of the aspiring presenter, and so is a willingness to accept virtually any job in a broadcasting organisation to get an 'in'. Phone answering, 'fact pack' envelope stuffing, studio audience ushering and news cuttings research are all on the 'pay your dues first' list of first jobs in broadcasting.

The news presenter Martyn Lewis says: 'I'd advise people to take the jobs no one else wants and make something of them. For example, when the job of Northern Correspondent was going at ITN, it was offered to all the other ITN reporters before myself, at that time the most junior. I took it and found that I was getting huge amounts of stories on air. I turned it into something very good; in the end I stayed in the job for seven and a half years.'

John Stapleton also realised that a period of 'paying his dues' would pay off in the end: 'After a spell in print journalism, I became a links writer on Thames's local evening news show. Once I had my feet under the table there, I volunteered for all the awful jobs that the reporters didn't want to do: vox pops at seven o'clock in the morning, late-night reports. So when one of the reporters left to go to another job, they gave me the post of full-time reporter. That was my big break on the screen and everything else followed from there.'

Gaining qualifications

A broad range of qualifications is certainly useful; as a broadcaster you'll have to be an instant expert on a surprisingly diverse selection of subjects. One day you may be putting together a feature on lava flow, the next day interviewing a surgeon about operation procedures. You should be able to absorb information accurately and quickly; remember there is no need to know too much. After all, you should be asking the kinds of questions the listeners or viewers themselves would want to ask and your interviewees should provide answers which make sense to the layman.

A balanced education and natural curiosity are what are required as a starting point for most reporting or feature work. But what if you want to specialise? If you have ambitions to get into television through research or production work, a degree is important — your chosen subject isn't. Studying for and attaining any degree shows that you have the ability to assimilate and to communicate detailed information; that you are used to asking and being asked questions. Most degree work consists of constant research, just like you would do at a TV station. Choose a subject which holds your interest; it also provides a peg upon which to hang a career in broadcasting. For example, a degree in politics would help your application to join a political programme's team; a degree in music would be a big advantage if you hoped to become a presenter on BBC Radio 3 or Classic FM.

People with a deep yearning to get stuck into broadcasting rarely stay on to study further than a first degree; any extra years in academia will in most cases be a waste of time unless you want to become a niche broadcaster. If you feel that your first degree grade could be bettered, don't worry – my advice is to get job hunting. An academic brain needs the catalyst of experience to transform the individual into a potent, employable broadcaster.

It is not the end of the world if you can't see yourself getting on a degree course. Maybe you are of the age where family commitments would make it financially difficult for you to become a student again. Good broadcasters are, at the end of the day, good communicators, and this comes from attending 'The University of Life'. A person who has experienced a broad range of situations, who has the confidence to talk to all kinds of people, to stand up for themselves on issues that they believe in, and who takes a keen and genuine interest in all kinds of current affairs, is the sort of person who will do well against blander applicants fresh out of college – however good their academic qualifications.

Lynn Parsons, of 1 FM, had an engineering background. She says, 'Having gained an OND in electrical engineering, I did a Principles of Television course at Leeds Polytechnic, and worked as a sound- and then a vision-mixer for TV-AM.' She always wanted to front a radio show and sent a showtape to Capital Radio in 1987 which resulted in a nightly three-hour show, before she moved to 1 FM.

Nicky Fox, co-presenter of ITV's *The Motor Show*, started her broadcasting career as an assistant film editor. 'I was cutting together children's programmes and documentaries at the BBC in London; I'd always liked to have had a go at on-screen work, but being stuck all day in a film editing room was not the ideal place to hear of opportunities.'

A friend of Nicky tipped her off that the then ITV breakfast service, TV-AM, was looking for another weather presenter. A few phone calls and letters later, she was offered an audition, which she passed. 'I ended up with Ulrika Jonsson and the team, and really enjoyed my first on-screen experience. We weather girls even got onto the cover of the *TV Times*!

'My advice would be: don't let any break go to your head and don't let any grass grow under your feet. At TV-AM, I volunteered to put together a regular travel feature, or "strand" for the station, which led to production work at the BBC's *Holiday* programme. You must always strike while the iron is hot. I remember waiting abroad with the film crew for the presenter, Anne Gregg, to arrive – her aeroplane was delayed. So instead of hanging around for hours doing nothing, I persuaded the crew to film me standing in for Anne on certain shots: close-ups of my hand on a wine glass, distant shots of me walking on the beach, that sort of thing.' Nicky's presentation work currently takes her to both sides of the Atlantic. She lives in America fronting news programmes and business videos and flies over to Britain to present projects such as *The Motor Show*.

In Chapter 12 we'll look at the qualifications a potential journalist or newsreader needs to attain. You'll find broadcasters with a variety of academic backgrounds: Anna Ford gained a degree in Social Anthropology and took a postgraduate diploma in Adult Education; Nick Ross graduated in Psychology; 1 FM's Mark Tonderai has a degree in Architecture! This is not to imply that you haven't a chance if you have few qualifications. After all, Chris Evans had big ambitions but, having left school with no useful certificates at all, he took a variety of jobs, including one as a private detective, before his personality and enthusiasm achieved far more than any qualification could do: 'I persuaded Timmy Mallett, who was then presenting on Manchester's Piccadilly Radio to take me on as a "helper". This meant answering the phone lines and doing a lot of running around and being silly in the studio.' His natural exuberance and originality shone through and on-air work soon followed. The contacts he made in a working radio station would have been essential, too, for him to talk to the right people about future opportunities.

'How much will it all cost?'

Your telephone calls will count up, but there are only two capital investments you ought to make before you start your quest for on-air work. If you are putting yourself forward as a professional presenter, you ought to present yourself in the best possible way. What lands on your potential boss's desk has got to 'look the business'. It has to create the right impression.

LETTERHEADS AND BUSINESS CARDS Simple, yet stylish. Something that sells you as a cool professional. £75–£100 should get you in business. If you have the extra investment money, personalised audio or video labels and inlay cards which match your letterhead will complete the professional look. Even if you are a school leaver, an individual 'designer' letterhead put together on a computer will show that you are a serious contender.

FACE THE FAX If you haven't got a fax machine at home, register at a local bureau so you can print its number on your letterhead to give a professional impression. This won't cost anything unless you start receiving faxes. Make sure its area code is the same as yours, so it looks as though you own a home office machine.

PHOTOGRAPHS   Photos are essential even for radio applications – you are trying to make an impression, remember, but a bad photograph can do you more harm than good. Seek out a professional who uses the 2¼ inch rather than 35mm format for better quality pictures. Ideally, he or she will specialise in showbusiness profiles. Order a colour version for printing off and a few black and white versions to send off for inclusion in directories such as *Spotlight, Showbase UK* or *Showcall Directory* which lists actors, presenters, and so on. Have a look at these handbooks in your library and notice the tricks other artists play with their images. Forget long shots, and don't worry too much about clothes; it's your *face* people will study. Decide on your image: zany, fun, happy, personable, authoritative or even stern, it's up to you. (We look more at clothing in Chapter 9, *The TV Presenter*.)

Tell the photographer the mood you want to convey and be prepared to spend between £100 and £200 for the session and prints. Find out if the fee includes the negatives; some photographers have a habit of upping the price when you need reprints. If you haven't the budget for professional pictures, find a keen amateur who can help you out. If he or she can work in black and white, so much the better; black and white gives a 'classier' image than reprints of domestic colour snaps.

Now you have created an image, armed with photos, letterheads and bags of determination, it's time for battle to commence.

'So, how do I get started?'

Target your sights. There's no use mailing out a general *'I think that I would like to work in Broadcasting'*-type letter, unless you're merely after general voluntary work such as answering the phone, or being a 'runner'. Go for work you know you will enjoy, *first*. For example, let's say that you enjoy watching a certain documentary TV series, and you feel that with your interests and background you would be an excellent on-screen reporter or at least a researcher on it. Find out who the editor or producer is, and type a letter. Don't make it too long, don't become flippant or 'chummy' and include sensible ideas for future programmes and how you feel they could be tackled. Be careful you don't word it *'Here's how I can improve your series'*; the right angle is *'If I were working with your team, here's what I would suggest for future projects'*.

Everybody loves new ideas, and don't worry that your thoughts will be stolen; after all, if an original idea of yours were used, you would be in an even better position to demand an interview at least.

If you are enquiring about presentation openings at radio and TV stations, it will help your case greatly if you enclose an audio or video showtape, with examples of your performances, in the style of the operation to which you are sending it. More on this later on. However, the paperwork you enclose with this cassette must be thought about very carefully. A photograph is essential; write your name and phone number on the back in case it gets separated from the rest of your package.

A good CV or Curriculum Vitae is essential to any job application, no matter how much extra material like tapes, pictures or press cuttings you include with it. It gives your potential employer an instant overview of your situation, experiences and talents. If you are worried that some of your work experience is irrelevant to broadcasting, word it so that it is angled in your favour. For example, a summer job in a burger bar may sound far more relevant to presentation when you mention that you won a commendation for organising and performing at children's parties.

There are many CV writing services around, but unless they really understand broadcasting, give them a wide berth, and do it yourself following my Top 10 rules of CV writing:

THE CV TOP TEN

☑ Produce it on a decent word processor and printer combination. Choose an easy-to-read font not smaller than 12 point, lay it out clearly, and print it out on the best quality paper you can afford.

☑ Put yourself inside the mind of your future boss. What does he or she want from you? Is the award-winning student film you worked on your biggest selling point? If so, then put it near the top. Are your age, address and marital status irrelevant to the application? Put this information near the end. List your career history with your most recent work experience first.

☑ Cut out any irrelevant words. Don't bother to type 'Curriculum Vitae' at the top; it's obvious what the document is. Your name should have top billing! Aim for a maximum of two pages.

☑ Sell, sell, sell. Banish any self-doubts and brag without resorting to arrogance. Eliminate the negative, accentuate the positive.

☑ Don't list irrelevant qualifications. If you have a degree there is no need to detail less important certificates. Just say '6 GCSEs' or whatever.

☑ Strike a good balance between simple, clear sentences and unpretentious 'buzz' words that will add zest and enthusiasm. Winning

CVs always seem to include words like: *ambition, creativity, determination, highly regarded, successful, career, qualities, experience, opportunities, leadership, award-winning, prestigious, upgrading, promotion, ratings-winning.*

☑ Clearly mark references to photographs, tapes, or news cuttings you have enclosed. These supplementary items may become separated from the main CV. Don't put rubber bands round cassettes attaching them to your CV; they will only be taken off, leaving your precious document crumpled.

☑ Check your CV contains enough positive experiences, qualifications and knowledge plus realistic ambitions for the future. Don't lie.

☑ Ask a friend or family member to check your CV once you've finished. They're bound to point out something which you've missed, not to mention spelling errors!

☑ Always give the reader of your CV plenty of reasons to invite you in for an interview or audition.

If you'd like further help and advice on producing your CV, *The Perfect CV* by Tom Jackson (Piatkus) is one of the best books around on the subject.

The covering letter should be very concise and tempt the recipient into wanting to find out more about your background. *Never* send a 'Dear Sir / Madam' letter. It only takes a telephone call to find out who you should be addressing and the correct spelling of their name. They may be sensitive about their actual job title, so ask about that too.

A very important word to use is 'opportunities' (e.g. an *opportunity* in radio presentation); media people tend to consider 'employment' or 'jobs' rather too vulgar terms to use. The words 'breaks' and 'chances' sound desperate.

Here is an example of a covering letter to a regional news editor of a radio or TV station asking for a non-advertised job as a junior newsroom assistant. This letter should sell you well enough for the recipient to want actually to read your CV. If you can afford to print it on your own letterhead, so much the better. It's important to make an impression, so think professional.

Note no actual job title is mentioned, because 'assistant' is a very vague term, and different newsrooms call juniors different things. Just sell your abilities and plant the idea that you would be a useful member of the team to have around. The sort of work you are angling for is for the job of runner / letter opener / fax operative / camera tripod carrier / camera crew driver / phone answerer / newspaper filer etc., but don't mention any of this in your letter.

This condensed selling style can be adapted to any job application.

(Correct name)
(Correct title)
(Correct address with postcode)

(Date)

Re: Opportunities in (Radio/TV station name newsroom)

Dear (Correct name)

I am writing to ask if you may be interested in my services in your newsroom. I was born and brought up in the region and know the area well. I have a clean driving licence, am computer literate and currently work in the offices of (local paper), where long hours and using initiative is the norm.

As you can see from my CV I used to work on a school magazine and have good English GCSE grades.

Could I meet you in the next few weeks to discuss opportunities?

Yours sincerely

(Your Name)

The follow-up

Follow up your postal enquiry with a telephone call, after three or four working days. Less than this would be unreasonable as the recipient may not have had time to read it; any longer and you may get sent a *'Sorry, no vacancies'*-type standard reply.

If you get the latter, you're rather stuck because what you really want to know is *why* there are no vacancies, when to try again, will there be any other openings, who else you should try, and so on. Once you get the finality of the *'Don't call us'* note, you may feel it difficult to open up the lines of communication again.

Getting through

The working hours of broadcasting management should be respected by you, the applicant. If you are calling a regional TV news operation, the editor usually chairs the morning ideas meeting and will not want to be disturbed. 11 o'clock should see them clear of this. 4 pm onwards, however, could see them involved with the editing of reports for that evening's news programme, and they are likely to be stressed and hassled.

Non-news TV producers tend to start very early and finish very late while a series is being made, balancing out the hours by showing up for only a few hours a day when putting together a new series. Radio management tends to work office hours of 9.30 to 6.

Let's assume that you're lucky and you get through straight away. Clearly state your name and reason for telephoning and enquire if your contact has had a chance to look at your correspondence. Angle to meet the person or to 'pop in' for a chat. Beware of being too pushy, the person could genuinely have no vacancies and your letter could have reached a decent filing system and not the bin. However, being reserved when you know you have talent to offer the programme or station is a crime. BBC's Martyn Lewis again: 'I would advise people still at school or university to go into their local radio station. Don't ring up, just go in... and don't go away until you've seen someone. People should be prepared to work for nothing for a while so that they can create opportunities where, at first glance, none would seem to exist. You need to be prepared for a long chain of refusals – fifty for every chance to do something.'

John Stapleton almost gave up hope of any work in the media when he first applied: 'I wrote to thirty-two papers and got thirty-two rejections; it was very demoralising.' Maybe if John had camped out in a few receptions rather than write letters, he might have had an earlier start.

What is important is to *make contact* and to get the impression across that you have the right qualities for the job. You must sound enthusiastic, knowledgeable and ask sensible questions about the station / programme / job ('opportunity'). On the telephone, try and sense the mood of the person at the other end of the line and react accordingly. If he or she is in a talkative mood, loosen up and push your luck a little if it will help you get a visit or interview.

If you sense that the person is wanting to get onto something else, wind the call up and get onto the *'Do you want to meet me?'* bit.

It is essential to log all letters and calls. When you are 'phone bashing', it is easy to forget who you called, when, and what was the result of that call. Don't be afraid to call every four weeks or so to ask politely if the situation has changed or if any vacancies are on the horizon. *Persistence, patience and continued enthusiasm do pay off.*

You have got to have the ability to sell yourself and seize every opportunity you can to maximise your chances. Keep your eyes and ears open for any leads to job opportunities. Children's TV presenter Sally Gray certainly goes along with that: 'There is an element of being in the right place at the right time in this business, but you also have to push yourself; you have to engineer your way in. It is a matter of luck, but you really have to go for it. People have a fear of the BBC, they think it is so big and unapproachable. But all you have to do is phone the main number and ask to go through to a specific department. Try to get chatting to a friendly secretary, pick up some advice, and, if necessary, be bolshy until you get to speak to the person you're after. Write in, send photos, do something wacky – anything that will get you noticed. Dress right wherever you go. Keep telling the people you meet what you want to do. Don't be shy, don't waste any time. Never think that you're not good enough because *you don't know unless you try.*'

How far can you go?

Some people seem to feel that the bizarre tactics adopted by record companies to plug their wares can be adapted to securing a job. I've known of audio cassettes being sent in cereal boxes for breakfast DJ jobs, calls to bosses' homes, outrageous faxes, and embarrassing gifts turning up on people's desks. All these are generally out of order, and will only serve to give the impression that you are an idiot to be avoided and not a potential professional broadcaster.

If you are not lucky enough to get through to your potential boss straight away, always get something positive out of the call. If you are informed that your contact is 'in a meeting', take Sally Gray's advice and open up a conversation with the secretary. After all, this person will know virtually everything there is to know about vacancies, qualifications, forthcoming new programmes and promotions. You can make a fool of yourself without jeopardising your chances with Mr / Ms Big. Impress the secretary and you've made an important step forward.

Don't forget that your research into future broadcasting careers need not just be done at the end of a telephone. There are plenty of media events, conferences and festivals where the people you need to contact can be found. The **Royal Television Society** has fifteen regional centres, all of which hold meetings and lectures. Some of these are open to the public. The **Edinburgh International Television Festival** is the venue for the annual pilgrimage of the industry, and the yearly **London Screenings** preview excerpts of forthcoming ITV and

Channel 4 programmes to executives and media students. There is an annual **Radio Festival**, organised by the Radio Academy, which consists of conferences, discussions and working sessions, and the latest equipment and programme technology is on show at the yearly **Television Show** in London. Contact addresses and/or phone numbers for all these bodies can be found in the Factfile on *Organisations* at the end of this book.

'Come in for a chat'

When you hear or read these wondrous words, you must grab the bull by both horns and make the most of the opportunity. Here is someone interested in you. You must *use* the meeting to sell yourself as a competent professional and to learn as much 'insider' information as possible: names, new programmes, promotions, anything could be useful to you.

Essential interview technique

☑ Arrive in reception a good fifteen minutes before your appointment. You'll get time to catch your breath, check how you look in the cloakroom mirror, read internal newsletters and noticeboards, and you might bump into someone who could help your cause.

☑ When collected by a secretary or whoever, use those valuable seconds on the way to the boss's office to enquire about the latest news at the TV or radio station. You might discover information about a new project and be able to impress your potential new boss that you're *au fait* with the current broadcasting world.

☑ Always accept the offer of a hot drink, even if you don't really want one. You'll be able to spin the interview out for longer, and a shared beverage always helps to break the ice.

☑ When beckoned into the lion's den, shake hands firmly while maintaining eye contact. Sit down only when asked to.

☑ Maintain 'open' body language. Arms folded and legs crossed show you are on the defensive as well as looking off-hand. Sit square and upright with your hands on your lap.

☑ Keep the eye contact with your potential new boss even though you're dying to scan the awards on the wall or the memos on the desk. Smile. Your face should look relaxed and receptive to questioning.

☑ Don't leave embarrassing 'thinking time' gaps after you're asked questions. Launch immediately into an enthusiastic buffer phrase while you think of the true direction of the answer. This is a favourite trick of politicians, who will instantly say things like: 'I'm SO glad you asked me that . . .' before starting the real answer.

☑ If your mind is getting addled by a barrage of questions, don't be afraid to turn the tables and ask some questions back. There must be plenty of things you want to know that show you have a professional interest in broadcasting. Before the interview, memorise three sensible questions you would like to ask.

☑ Towards the end of the 'audience', glance at a list of points you will have written previously. Is there anything else you need to get across? Do you need to ask anything else?

☑ Always end the session by taking your application forward. Never leave things in the air. You must keep the lines of communication open. Offer to come in and 'help out' for free, to bring in a new showtape, or agree to keep in touch every month or so.

☑ When you're finally shown the door, find somewhere quiet to write notes on all that's been said, before you forget.

1 *FM'S SIMON MAYO* made his first 'radio' programme at the age
of eight on the family tape-recorder (for some reason under the
name of Simon Stephens) with his sister doing jingles on the xylophone. Mark Thorburn of Metro FM in Newcastle admits that much
of his early teenage years was spent 'talking to himself' in his bedroom
on his homemade radio station.

Yes, radio is an industry where the bug usually bites early. Many
people who are now professionally behind the microphone decided to
get into the business when they were pretty young. They probably
grew up glued to their sets noting every slight change in DJ line-up or
even the mix of a jingle. This kind of obsession is one which can
develop into a curious condition, where the sufferers stand in all
weathers outside radio stations in their anoraks, waiting to meet presenters and their star guests. Radio staff learn to deal with this by
developing *anoraknophobia*, and sneaking out of the back door.

I am amazed how many people outside broadcasting assume that
music radio presenters come from the 'clubs'. Disco DJs and radio DJs
may be playing similar music, but they have completely different skills
and personalities and are usually not very good at doing each other's
jobs. A Disco DJ may be excellent at live mixing, choosing the song
sequence, rousing the crowd and organising games and stunts, but be
completely at sea in a radio studio where there is no visual element and
no crowd to play off. Of course the opposite is true, and the best music
radio presenter can look a real fool out of the security of the soundproofed studio under the glare of a club's lighting bank with someone
else at the controls. When it comes to speech-based radio such as
Radio 4, BBC local radio or the few commercial ·speech stations,

presenters would normally have come from the ranks of journalism, especially if they have to deal with current affairs interviews and phone-ins. More on this later.

How they got their break

Radio Forth's Jay Crawford must be one of the luckiest people in radio. 'In 1974 I sent in a tape to Radio Forth prior to the station going on-air. I'd never worked as a DJ, I really didn't have a clue. They took a chance on me and I started off on six shows a week!' Jay is still at Forth twenty years later, so he must be doing something right.

Not everyone can expect to be signed up on his or her first application and you really need to use your 'nous' to get your foot in the door. For example, Red Dragon's Bobby McVay was a dancer in a panto in Cardiff: 'A local radio presenter was in the show and whetted my appetite for radio. I visited the station, and thought – I could do that!' Bobby made his contacts at the station fairly unconventionally: 'My first break into radio was helped by trying to chat up a stunning radio station sales rep in Tesco's car park. It was a way of getting to know who did what on her station, and what opportunities were on the horizon.'

The important thing to keep in mind is that the people we hear on radio or see on TV are not 'special people'. They are men and women who have a job to do and stay in that job by doing it well. If you can prove you can do a job equally well, you'll be given a chance. Compiling a showtape is one way of doing this. We'll look at how to make the most effective tape in the next chapter.

Today's professional presenters have a wide variety of experience. Steve Wright's first job was as a shelf stacker in a supermarket, although he caught the radio bug after running the internal radio station at Eastwood High School in Essex. A variety of jobs including insurance broker and theatre backstage worker did nothing to appease this urge. 'My first job in radio was presenting my own show on a pirate radio station, Radio Atlantis. I recorded the shows in my home studio and sent the tapes out to the ship for broadcasting.' Steve got his first terrestrial break at Reading's Radio 210 as a news reporter, and worked at London's LBC before getting his own show in Reading. After a stint at Luxembourg, he joined Radio 1 in 1980.

Mark Tonderai's love of music didn't pay the bills and, after graduating as an architect, he worked as a cycle courier, fishmonger and a teacher on a project for disadvantaged children before becoming a successful applicant on a BBC positive action scheme, funded by the

Network Radio Equal Opportunities Office. If you are a member of an ethnic minority, it is worth contacting the Office at Broadcasting House in London.

One route into hosting your own radio show is via traffic report presentation. Some radio stations have these bulletins provided by a service such as AA Roadwatch who have offices and studios around the UK connected by audio line to studios; others have dedicated staff based in-house.

Helen Briggs now has her own regular programmes on the North West regional station JFM 100.4 after proving her worth presenting traffic bulletins. 'Travel news writing and presentation isn't exactly an easy option. For example, I cover the huge North West region and I have to make regular calls to a long list of police control rooms and other contacts. I then have to assimilate the information quickly and condense it into ninety-second bulletins which I read on air three times per hour. There is usually not enough time to write out a full script, and so I have taught myself to ad lib, sometimes about information which is passed to me while I am actually on air. You have to explain traffic jams and travel problems clearly and with authority; you have to get it right, as a listener who is given incorrect information might be one listener lost to the radio station. I'd say it's excellent training to be a main radio presenter.'

So how did she make the transition to fronting her own radio programme? 'I took advantage of the situation of being based in the radio station rather than working in some remote office where you never meet radio station staff. I made myself known, got to hear of a few programme changes that were coming up, and took the opportunity of booking some studio time in order to make demo tapes, to prove to the management that I could do the job. I also taught myself to read the regional news as well as to learn to operate the control desk. You have to use your initiative, and quickly grasp opportunities to get on.'

Alison Brown, the daily afternoon presenter of BBC Radio Lancashire based in Blackburn, agrees. 'After a spell typing out "what's ons" at the station, I was asked last year to step in and read traffic bulletins and it all started from there. It's funny, but it's only after people hear your voice on a loudspeaker that they make comments on it, even though they hear me every day in the office. It was a huge leap from reading out traffic jams to hosting my own afternoon programme, interviewing everybody from chefs to captains of industry. It all happened so quickly and I was fairly apprehensive initially. You are on a steep learning curve and you mustn't be afraid to ask for help from established broadcasters.'

Alison's background is as a production assistant (PA) in television, but this has been her first break on air. 'I may go back to television work one day, but my radio programme can be so satisfying. On BBC local radio you're not just spinning discs; there is also plenty of interesting speech content. You are interviewing local people about local issues – it's more of a public service than pure entertainment and the job is extremely rewarding.'

At the other end of the country, Monica Ellis at BBC Radio Devon enjoys similar on-air work to Alison Brown. When Monica was working out her career plan at school, she knew that further education would be essential in pursuing her ambition of working in speech radio. 'I appreciated that the competition to get into the BBC was very fierce, so after gaining A-levels, I embarked on a social science degree course. A large part of the course involved politics and human geography – the sorts of things that I thought would be useful in speech broadcasting. When my course was coming to an end I wrote to virtually every BBC department and local radio station. Even though my qualifications were pretty spot on, I was advised to gain some experience: the typical Catch 22 situation. My break actually came via the Community Service Volunteers. CSV Media have offices round the country tying in volunteers with social action broadcasting. One such scheme in Plymouth gave me the opportunity to work at BBC Radio Devon. I made the most of every minute – I watched, I learned, I worked. I knew I had to broaden my experience to be employable. Eventually I ended up with a real paid job! I operated the control desk for the breakfast show, researched features for the mid-morning programme and worked on reception. I even put together the weekend request show. I now present regular daily programmes on BBC Radio Devon and the work is satisfying and very interesting.'

Monica's advice to prospective speech radio applicants is this: 'Education is all; each week you will be expected to pick up background knowledge on a hundred and one different subjects with speed and be able to discuss them intelligently on air. You have to have empathy with both your interviewees and listeners.'

If you are well established in another industry, but have always had a yearning to be behind a microphone for a living, you can still create your own opportunities. David Way worked in the finance section of a bank for over fifteen years. The job offered financial security, but ever since he was a teenager he had wanted to work in the uncertain, sometimes crazy broadcasting industry. The Alton area in Hampshire was not properly served at the time by any local radio station, and David started a campaign group to set one up. He now has his own four-hour daily programme and, in addition, is the

Managing Director and Programme Controller of the radio station! 'My age and experience in finance helped our application in many ways. After all, a commercial radio station is a business, not just a vehicle for an ego trip. Wey Valley 102 was formed after we proved to the Radio Authority that there was a real need for a local radio station based in Alton. A temporary RSL (Restricted Service Licence) station we ran was very successful and we raised the capital to run a full service.'

If you feel that *your* local area is lacking its own radio station, or lacking a *type* of service none of the existing services provide, the Radio Authority may issue you with a licence for one of these short-run stations to test the water for a permanent set-up. More on Wey Valley later in this chapter, when we investigate volunteering opportunities.

Getting your foot through the door

Unlike TV stations and TV production companies, radio stations are run on much tighter budgets, have a generally higher turnover of staff and are usually more open to offers of 'helping out'. If you have little financial commitment in life, you have nothing to lose by working for free at one of your local radio stations. Offer to help out with their summer promotions on the road, giving stickers out, keeping people off the stage, and filing the roadshow records. Ask to help in the newsroom during routine calls or give a hand during the sports programme. There are always people needed to do odds and ends on Saturday afternoons during the soccer season.

How about a job in the record library? Tedious, but it's a way in. Ask if any presenter needs help answering the telephones. This way, you will see how programmes are put together at the sharp end. You will get to know the people involved and what they do, how the equipment is operated and what it all does. You will discover how much (or how little) a radio presenter puts into the programmes.

Contact the relevant programme editor or controller, using all the ploys I talked about in the previous chapter. Sound enthusiastic in your letter, and knowledgeable about its output, but not like an 'anorak'! This sort of thing is fine: *'I was particularly impressed by your One-Two-Free promotion; and your new travel bulletins are much easier to understand...'* This sort of thing is NOT: *'While I'm working for you, could I make a cassette copy of those Turbo Z jingles you have for my friends, although of course, they're not as good as the WBLS New York originals. . .'*

If you are offered voluntary work, learn as much as you can without getting in the way. After a while, you will get to know what job you would like to do on the station or decide instead that it's not the life for you.

Offer to do work in as many different departments as possible. Even if you want to be a presenter all your life, learning everybody else's jobs will help you understand the structure of a station and will let you appreciate other people's responsibilities. And if by chance you decide you eventually want to become a radio station manager, you will need to know the workings of the sales department, commercial traffic department, engineering, record library and promotions departments as well as programming.

It is important to strike a balance between working for free to gain experience and being taken advantage of. Wey Valley 102 in Alton was the first commercial radio station in the UK to rely heavily on volunteers. David Way, the Managing Director and Programme Controller: 'Apart from myself, most of the other presenters are volunteers. Since we cover such a small area, that was the only way that the station could survive financially. I don't feel as if I'm taking advantage of people; after all they are getting valuable experience on a radio station that is actually transmitting to this area of Hampshire. Some of my presenters have found paid work at larger stations after a spell here; this leaves a vacancy for another volunteer. It's an excellent situation and I believe that this system could be a blueprint for the future of small commercial stations.' So look out for on-air opportunities at local and community stations near you. The Radio Authority will be pleased to send you a free copy of their *Pocket Book* which details all the stations under their wing.

Paying your dues

Volunteering is possible for some, but what if you can only take advantage of opportunities that pay real money? If you're technically competent, a job as a trainee engineer, technical operator, studio manager or technical assistant would be a good start for a potential presenter, since you would get to know the operation of the desk and other equipment intimately without having to worry about what to say. Medium to large ILR and BBC local stations as well as the networks use people like this to 'drive' live or recorded shows. I know many TOs (technical operators) who have been rewarded by a daily show after serving a solid apprenticeship operating the studio desk.

Steve Penk of Piccadilly Key 103 is a good case in point: 'I joined the station as a trainee in the commercial production department and became a technical operator. One programme I drove on-air was a continuous music show, Magic Music, and when it was decided to include live links in the show, I volunteered to record a demo and have been on-air regularly ever since.' Steve Penk has certainly paid his dues, and now hosts the top-rated daily breakfast show on Key 103.

Promotions may be another way into radio. If you have skills in organising events like school society meetings, student union activities, etc, and are good at wheeling and dealing, a promotions assistant job may be right up your street. At outside broadcasts (OBs) and promotions at public shows, there is always need for a 'warm-up' DJ before the star turn comes on. This is where you will get your experience.

Remember that people are forever moving jobs in broadcasting, and the best people have many different skills in different areas. A news reporter may become news editor, and may in turn become a programme controller, or even chief executive. A sales assistant may become a sales executive or may join the commercial production department. Presenters may work in commercial production or promotions as well as doing their own programmes. As I always say, the more you can offer anyone, the more you will be valued, the more secure your job will be and the more money you can negotiate. It's as simple as that.

If you are new to broadcasting, you may have to set your sights lower before you get a break as a radio presenter. You may have to pay your dues first as a phone-in operator, technical operator, record librarian, promotions assistant, or whatever. You'll find on smaller stations that each person tends to do quite a few jobs, especially lower down the ladder. This situation is excellent for newcomers, because you learn so much about different areas.

One person may present the very early wake-up show, then answer telephones for the breakfast programme, before going out to conduct some interviews for the afternoon show, coming back to edit them, and leaving about 2 pm. Another may work part-time in the record library, and produce and present one or two specialist shows in the week. Someone else may go out with the radio car in the morning presenting news reports, then do an afternoon shift as technical operator in the newsroom, and do occasional promotion work for evening events at clubs. It's all down to the old 'being useful' rule again, which will give maximum job security and helps to pave the way for future career moves.

Let's detail four radio station jobs which may give you that first break into broadcasting:

PHONE-IN OPERATOR   This involves sitting in the phone-in room or studio annexe taking calls and routeing them on-air. You'll say 'Hello, QFM?' a hundred times a day. Although this may sound as if you're just a dogsbody, you are actually very important since you will talk to and deal with listeners far more than the programme controller or even the presenters. You'll know how well a feature is going down and get a true feel of the success of the station, as well as having the responsibility of contributing to the editorial content of a programme. The downside is little or no pay, and there may be long, unsociable hours.

Your job will involve:

■ Taking requests and dedications, then when the phone-in lines are opened, sussing out articulate, intelligent callers, keeping them on hold or calling them back when required.

■ Informing the producer or presenter who is on which line and what they would like to discuss on-air. You may have a computer keyboard on which to type this information, so that it appears on the studio screen, or you might quietly have to take pieces of paper in when the microphone is on.

■ Explaining the procedures to callers; telling them that they'll hear the programme down the telephone, asking them to switch off or turn down any radio to prevent 'howlround', and so on.

■ After the caller has been on-air, thanking them for their contribution, taking their address if they've requested information or have won a prize, and clearing the line.

■ Refusing boring regular callers without causing offence: 'Sorry, all our calls are booked for today.'

TECHNICAL OPERATOR / TECHNICAL ASSISTANT
These people are the backbone of any good radio station. Reporting to the programme controller and sometimes also to the chief engineer, they will know how to operate every tape machine and control desk in the building as well as knowing how to work all the radio cars and mobile radio backpack transmitters.

TOs are usually on some sort of duty roster, but life can be extremely varied and highly rewarding even if you don't get your voice on-air at first. Many TOs with good voices who want to become presenters do achieve their ambitions because they're so good at 'driving desks'. You'll enjoy great responsibility and variety. It's a chance to play with every knob and gadget in the building and it's a good springboard to production and presentation jobs. TOs normally have some kind of college certificate in electrical engineering, but an active interest in audio gear, hi-fi and recording is important too. Work experience at a music recording studio is a big plus point.

Your duties may be:

■ Operating the live on-air control desk while an outside broadcast is going on. You have the OB (outside broadcast) van or radio car output on a desk fader, and simply mix music, commercials and news bulletins as required by the producer, who may be in the studio with you or at the end of a 'talkback' line. The job needs initiative – especially, for example, when you hear something like this from your presenter down the talkback from location: *'Don't come to me after this record, my guest has run off . . . pad with something . . . ANYTHING!!'*

■ Driving the desk during a live or recorded discussion programme, where the presenter or interviewer isn't in a position to operate equipment as well.

■ Working in the newsroom 'carting up' stories coming from external news services, reclaiming tape, charging up portable tape-recorders, or carrying out a whole host of other duties that reporters or news editors feel are beneath them.

In one day you may find yourself responding to a great variety of requests: *'Can you drive my interview with Megadeth?'* (the rock DJ); *'Can you go out and operate my week-long OB from Florida?'* (the programme controller); *'Can you make cassette copies of these commercials?'* (the head of sales); *'Can you come home sometime?'* (your family).

RECORD LIBRARIAN   Not as daunting or boring as it might sound. In the old days, you would have had to log out and log back every record, and re-file piles and piles of them in the correct places. These days, most songs will be in Compact Disc jukeboxes or physically in the on-air studio, and the entire playlist will be entered into a computer. Only requests or specialist songs are now sought out along the racks and shelving. If you love music, and want to hear all the latest releases before they are in the shops, this is the job for you. If you're into computers as well, you will almost certainly enjoy it.

On the downside, however, is a potentially boring routine. You'll also discover that station staff will plead with you for free copies of records which aren't yours to give away, and you'll have to deal with endless calls from record companies plugging their wares.

Your duties:

■ Working for the head of music and updating the music computer. The software selects the order of songs and sticks to any commands which you programme in, such as listing a strong uptempo record to follow each news bulletin, giving three ballads an hour, making sure that no two female vocalists are played next to each other, etc.

■ Making sure the forms for the Performing Rights Society (PRS) and Phonographic Performance Limited (PPL) are filled in correctly and sent off weekly. This ensures that the writers of the songs (via the PRS) and the record companies (via the PPL) get their royalties from every song played on-air. These used to be hand-written, but now a computer will print out most of these details at the push of a button.

■ Receiving from record reps and through the post all the new releases for the weekly playlist meeting. You have them ready for this friendly shouting match where all the presenters are told by the head of music that they can't have their favourite records on the station playlist. You then enter the final, decided list into the computer, along with record number, duration, intro/talkover time, 'fade', 'cold fade' or 'ends' information and log details like artist, writer(s), publisher(s) and index numbers.

■ Keeping the library tidy and organised so that everyone can find things quickly. Maintaining security so discs aren't snaffled by kleptomaniac DJs and producers.

PROMOTIONS ASSISTANT Although not ideal as a springboard to on-air work, this job will give you a lot of experience in organising things and communicating clearly with people. You'd work with the promotions manager in putting together outside broadcast events in liaison with the programming department, arranging publicity stunts and exhibitions, as well as being involved with station-sponsored concerts and events. It's a job which is great for getting involved and becoming partly responsible for the success of out-of-studio activities, promoting the radio station to the public.

Your duties:

■ A lot of running and driving around (clean licence essential), delivering artwork of publicity brochures or stickers to printers and collecting finished goods. You may have to carry boxloads of promotional shirts and mugs to roadshow locations, where you'll put up the radio station's banner and posters, taking them all down again after the event.

■ Doing 'recces' of locations for future events, checking powerpoints, radio car signal strength, access and safety barrier requirements, and so on. Liaising with managements of clubs, halls, shopping precincts, etc, and keeping them sweet.

■ Installing PA (public announcement) or disco equipment on the day, and checking everyone knows what they're doing, so it all runs smoothly. You may have to 'warm up' the audience before the show starts; this is of course good experience if your eventual aim is to be on-air.

Hospital radio

Over 11,000 volunteers are involved with hospital radio in the UK, and are based at over 300 radio stations. Hospital radio stations are not commercially operated, there are no adverts or sponsorship credits, nor can the broadcast programmes normally be heard outside the hospitals. Programmes are normally relayed to the wards via cables from a studio which feeds into the bedside headphones of the patients.

The aim of hospital broadcasting is to entertain and inform, to help relieve the feeling of isolation and boredom most people encounter in hospital. The radio station becomes, to the patient, a link with the outside world beyond the medical or nursing staff, and therefore not connected with their illness.

Hospital radio also encourages participation from patients, helping them to get to know their fellow patients and develop a ward 'team spirit'. Stations vary from small set-ups which broadcast only through the evenings, to multi-studio stations with enough volunteers on tap to put out programmes throughout the day and night. There are even a small but growing number of hospital television stations which make programmes wired to monitors in the wards.

Many former hospital radio broadcasters can now be found working in professional TV and radio concerns, and gained their initial training behind the hospital radio microphone. The Hospital Broadcasters' Association (HBA) – previously known as The National Association of Hospital Broadcasting Organisations (NAHBO) – can give you more information and tell you who to contact in your area, if you'd like to get involved.

Pirate radio

Just forget it. It may be very easy to construct or buy a broadcast transmitter and set it up in a bedroom or a field, but what's the point? You'll lose a lot of money when the gear is confiscated, even more when the fine has to be paid, and you'll be shunned by the professional radio industry. You'll be *persona non grata* in the Radio Authority's eyes.

The law has tightened up a lot since Steve Wright started out recording tapes for Radio Atlantis and since the pioneering days in the 1960s when it was perfectly legal to transmit outside of territorial waters. Of course we have the pirates to thank for many of the top names in UK radio – Tony Blackburn, the late Kenny Everett, Dave Cash, Roger Day – but this is history now.

There are now more legal radio stations than ever in the UK, so there are plenty of opportunities, as long as you sell yourself in the right way, using the information in this book. If you get frustrated by what seem to be endless rejection letters, take heart – everyone has a file of these somewhere. Talent rises to the top eventually; and talentless charlatans who get offered shows by their friends in the boss's chair always get found out when the poor ratings come in.

CHAPTER 4

THE RADIO SHOWTAPE

*Y*OU THINK YOU'RE GOOD. Your friends and your family think you're good. How can you persuade a programme controller to hire you as a radio presenter?

A neat letter and appropriate CV will prise the door open a little, but to get through it completely, you will need to produce a stunning audition tape. Don't panic. Programme controllers receive many of these tapes every week, but when I had this job for a spell, I couldn't believe how badly many of them were put together. There is plenty of scope to make yours stand out above the others as original and professional. Unlike theatrical auditions, which are live, you can easily re-record over your mistakes and hone and craft the best audition tape possible.

'What needs to go into the tape?'

A good variety of *types* of links; in Chapter 6 you'll find plenty of ideas to choose from, but remember that the radio station wants to hear just *you*. Forget the records, commercials and news bulletins. Choose half a dozen songs which roughly match the style of the station you're aiming at, but don't worry too much about the choice. Leave a record playing for about three or four seconds after you've introduced it, then edit to the last four seconds. The rougher the edit the better; your potential employer will then know the tape has been 'telescoped' all the way through. Why send a whole hour of a finished programme, so the listener has the annoyance of fast forwarding to find your links? Everybody knows the songs – *you* are the unknown quantity.

The whole tape should be no longer than five minutes – leave them wanting more. Send it on a high-quality chrome cassette (not metal, because if played on a machine that hasn't been adjusted, it will sound muffled) and label it clearly and neatly, including your name and contact numbers. You can send a duplicate on the professional reel-to-reel format or on Digital Audio Tape (DAT) if you wish, but it is almost certain that the cassette version will be the one listened to.

'What station do I announce?'

If you send a cassette to a local BBC or commercial radio station and on the cassette you pretend to be on 1 FM, it is likely to be viewed as if you would rather work for the national station, and would have no commitment to the station you've contacted. Sending a tape of a mock-up show on a station which is obviously a direct rival is right out. Why insult the programme controller, who may actually think you are a good presenter? (If you have some genuine recordings of your work on another station, that is another matter. Send the best ones you have.)

Custom tapes

My answer would be to target a few stations you think you have a good chance of getting work with and produce custom tapes just for them. A word of warning: don't give any timechecks. If, for example, you pretend to be on a station's breakfast show, it will look as if you are angling for the job of the current presenter. You will be sending your tape to the boss who probably *chose* the current presenter, so leave timechecks out and let him or her decide what time of day or night you would be best suited for. A friendly engineer or technical operator at the station may dub off some jingles to help you to compile the tape, but this is not important.

Mailshot tapes

If you are sending out the same cassette to a large number of stations, don't identify any station at all. It's logical when you think about it; after all, it's *your* voice, personality, and the way *you* say things that are the most important aspects of your audition tape.

'What name do I use?'

A name is a very subjective thing, but if you have a name similar to that of an established radio presenter, maybe you should adopt a 'stage name'. If you can carry it off, why not a completely fictitious appellation, like Dwerton F. Beesley, or Sheel Moot Egg? It'll get you noticed! (I personally can't stand stage names which are two first names, like Paul Christopher or David Wayne: it's such a *passé* '70s' thing.)

'What will radio stations be looking for?'

■ Someone who will complement their current roster of presenters – are you a female who could enhance an all-male station? Or could you handle a late-night phone-in?

■ A personality which sounds natural, and not obviously copied from someone else.

■ A certain standard of intelligence, and an awareness of life's problems.

■ A clear voice which is easy to listen to.

■ That indefinable, potential 'star quality', which transforms a well-balanced, confident individual into a professional broadcaster.

'Where do I record my showtape?'

The ideal situation is for you to have a home studio, where you can be relaxed and make mistakes without fear of embarrassment. A professional microphone and a stage mixer connected to a decent Hi-Fi sound system might be good enough in a room with 'dead' acoustics – heavy curtains or whatever – to absorb sound reflections. Next best is your local hospital radio station, where you might be volunteering anyway. Otherwise, be prepared to spend about £50 an hour for a commercial recording studio. Look up the adverts in the 'Recording Services – Sound' section of the *Yellow Pages*; some studios specialise in recording radio audition tapes.

Avoiding the main pitfalls

■ Obtain other opinions. Make sure you play your tape to friends and family for their objective and honest opinions. You may have missed the fact that all your links have '*you know*' in them, or that you're gabbling too fast for comprehension.

■ Wait until you're sure. Don't send your tape until you are really happy with it. In the same way that top record producers rarely mix down a song from the multitrack recorder on the day they record it, leave your tape unposted for a day or so and then listen to it again. All sorts of imperfections rear their ugly heads in the cold light of day. An annoying slur of a word, a punchline that didn't quite work, a link that went on too long... Hone! Polish! Re-record! It's important to get the first tape as good as possible. After all, why should a programme controller bother to listen to an improved cassette you mail at a later date if you didn't come across well on the first?

■ Don't forget the paperwork. Enclose with the cassette a neatly typed covering letter along with a relevant CV. If you have no broadcasting experience to talk about, forget the CV and put in a sheet of relevant interests. A photo is important to make an impression – no matter what kind of broadcasting work you are applying for. So make an impression!

■ Follow up! Your cassette may impress, yet no vacancies may exist at the moment. Radio station bosses are only human and may have forgotten you in a few months' time when an opportunity actually arises. Make an appointment, and aim for an informal meeting so you get to meet the boss face to face. Be professional – keep in touch regularly, but don't hassle. If you really want a job on-air, you must be prepared to do these things.

CHAPTER 5

THE RADIO STUDIO
and how to operate it

CYNICS IN THE INDUSTRY say that there are usually two types of self-operated radio studios: those that have been designed by programme controllers, and those that have been designed by engineers.

The programmer's ideal studio design contains only the controls you actually need. The studio is designed with simplicity of operation, robustness and ergonomics in mind. There are spaces to put scripts and CDs; cartridge or digital-storage fire buttons are in the same line-of-sight as the machines themselves; and faders are clearly marked and in a logical order.

The engineer's studio, on the other hand, looks more like a cross between the flight decks of the USS *Enterprise* and Concorde; that is, both impressive and over-budget. The desk is similar to a rig designed for complicated music or advertisement recording where virtually every parameter of sound can be altered. Equalisation (bass, middle and treble), pan (left and right), mono (mix of left and right), reverberation (a type of echo) and phase shift buttons are available on every channel.

I know that at this stage of your career you won't have much control over the design of your radio studio, but do me a favour, will you? One day when you're sitting in that plush office with the 'Programme

Controller' plaque on your door, get your chief engineer in and work out the best design for your needs *together*.

For this section I am going to assume you have never been in front of a radio desk (also known as a console) before. The first thing to remember is that virtually anyone can get the hang of operating a radio studio. If you ever feel overwhelmed or daunted by it all, just sit back, take a deep breath, think of the radio presenter you despise the most and say out loud: 'If that idiot can operate a desk, there is no reason why I can't as well.'

Faders

A fader is really a linear volume control which you push up and down to make the sound heard from a sound source louder or softer. A sound source can be a record deck, CD player, tape machine, microphone or outside source (such as the radio car). Each sound source will have its own dedicated circuits, or 'channel', on the radio desk, and its own fader on that channel, so you can control the total output of the desk. In other words, the faders you select, and their position, determine the level and mix of sound to go on the studio tape-recorder or on the air.

On BBC radio desks, when the fader is fully 'up', the source is off, and when the fader is fully 'down', the sound is at maximum volume. On most commercial stations and recording studios it is the other way around. In other words, you push the fader of the appropriate source *up* to get a noise.

The thinking behind this variation is very curious. Legend has it that a (now long-pensioned-off) BBC engineer thought that if operators collapsed on-air (like you do), then they would slump forward and push the faders off, giving a respectful silence on-air to mark their demise. Of course, in advertiser-conscious commercial radio, everyone is so paranoid about listeners switching off in any slight gap that the faders are reversed, so a dead operator would slump forward and open up a cacophony of sound. Listeners would think they were tuning into the latest bizarre dance song, the old DJ would be dragged out, a new one installed and everyone would be happy and none the wiser.

Trim / Gain controls

These can be used in conjunction with faders. Usually found at the top of each channel, these should give you more volume if you're playing a soft record with the fader fully open. Likewise, you may need to turn down a particularly noisy source if it is causing distortion.

Start / Stop buttons

These simply start and stop the relevant sources and are usually located at the top of the faders. You may have a choice between 'manual start' and 'fader start'. With manual start, you cue up, say, a CD track, then put the fader on. When you need the song to start, you push the start button. With fader start, the action of taking the fader away from the end-stop (and triggering a microswitch) starts the source.

Personally, I don't like the fader start option. I like to keep the fader of the next source I want to use open so when I am talking on air I can see it out of the corner of my eye. This acts as a reminder, so that I don't push a wrong button. In addition, the song may have a loud or soft start, and with manual start you can adjust the fader accordingly beforehand. If you do prefer fader start, be aware that songs cued up on this system tend to start playing without your noticing if you carelessly nudge the fader just off the end-stop.

Prefade / Prefade-listen (PFL) / Prehear / Solo

Don't worry, they're all different names for the same concept. There will be one of these switches for each source and it will enable you to listen to a source without it going to master desk output and thus to air.

You need to cue up vinyl discs and CDs, listen to commercials or tapes to check out cues, and to check that your satellite news or OB vehicle is coming in loud and clear. Flicking a prefade switch usually dims the volume of the speakers, and there may be another switch so you can listen solely to what you're prefading without a mix with the on-air signal.

If the speakers won't go loud enough or the meters do strange things, always check that you haven't accidentally pushed one of these buttons before calling the engineer.

Desk / Off-air switch

Unless it really puts you off listening to a hissy FM or muffled AM signal, always do your programme listening 'off-air' and *not* directly from the output of the desk. The off-air switch will give you what is actually broadcast after going through all the gear in the lines room and transmitter. Listening 'off the radio' will sharpen your concentration and keep the adrenalin going if you're feeling tired. It will also tell you if the transmitters are working properly. I know of a few occasions where the radio presenter has carried on with the show oblivious of the fact that the transmitter had actually stopped working!

Meters

Forget what anyone may tell you about magical 'compressors' and 'Optimod' machines taking care of your sound levels. Forget also about trying to make your show 'louder' than the others by bending the needles off the end-stops of the meters. Discipline in maintaining correct levels will really pay off in keeping distortion at bay and maintaining relative levels between different sound sources.

For example, if you peak a song at 6 on the meter and peak your voice at only 4, the listener will have a job to hear what you're saying. Music is usually processed through a device called a compressor to make it sound 'louder' anyway. Some radio stations have their own rules on this, but a good guide is to peak all recorded music at 4, commercials, promos and jingles at 5 and live voice at 6. You will find these numbers on the PPM or Peak Programme Meter. Outside the UK, you will find VU or Volume Unit meters in widespread use. If you have these, ask your engineer how they are lined up to equivalent PPM settings.

Talkback switches

These let you communicate with other studios – the newsroom, for example – without going to air. Check where the talkback microphone is. It may be the master microphone or a tiny capsule on the other side of the desk.

Record decks

CDs and CD jukeboxes may have taken over in recent years, but there will be a place for the vinyl record in a radio studio for quite a while

to come. Remember to keep your greasy fingers off the playing sur-
faces. Grease and static do attract the dirt that clogs the grooves. If an
often-played record is in bad condition, ask the technical people to cut
out the crackle and hiss with a graphic equaliser, then put it on a tape
cart or on DAT cassette. Also, once you've cued a record, don't keep
on cueing to make sure. Endless motions back and forth wear out the
first few inches of a disc and cause a horrible *kkhhhrr!* sound. This is
called 'cueburn'.

CD players

Compact Disc has many advantages over vinyl, but the main plus for
a radio station is that you can cue a song anywhere you like, and it will
come in clean. Try this with vinyl and you have to be careful not to
'wow' in the music as the turntable rumbles up to speed. Using CD
allows you to cut out a boring soft start of a song and cue it exactly
where something interesting happens: perfect for difficult segue work,
where you have to play a softer song after a loud one. Set the display
to count *down* rather than count *up*. The presenter needs to know how
long a song has to go rather than how long it has played. Don't trust
the counter on unfamiliar songs: 00.00 isn't always the end of the
track. I have known songs end suddenly at minus 15 seconds or so! Be
prepared: check first.

CD jukeboxes

Sixty or more CDs are stored in each machine, locked away from the
kleptomaniac clutches of the presenters. A computer terminal in the
studio, with appropriate software, plays the songs. There are no CD
box inserts to read and there is no temptation to play an alternative,
personal favourite track.

Tape machines

The professional open-reel system uses ¼-inch magnetic tape running
at a speed of 7½ or 15 inches per second. The format is 'full track',
which means all the width of the tape is used up in one direction. You
can't turn the reels over as you can with cassettes.

There are two main equalisation systems you may encounter, NAB
and IEC. Don't worry too much if you push the button by mistake, the

switch only makes a slight tone difference. Radio tapes rarely have Dolby encoding.

Other switches on the tape machine may include reel size. This tells the machine whether you have heavy metal reels or light plastic spools, and will help to run the tape smoothly over the heads, and prevent it from stretching. Always prefade a reel-to-reel tape (listen without it going on-air), before playing it on-air. You may find it wound backwards (known as 'tail out') to minimise the effect of long-term 'print-through' (where sounds come through too early, like 'shadows'). Even more confusing, you may find the sound doesn't directly follow the leader tape as it should, but comes several ghastly seconds after it. Wind through the reel and check that the out cue and duration given to you are correct.

Cartridge machines

Now being replaced by digital storage systems, the tape cartridge system is a method for playing jingles, promos and commercials. These plastic-shelled cartridges ('carts') contain an endless loop of ¼-inch magnetic tape in various lengths. The most popular lengths are 20, 40, 70, 90, and 100 seconds, 3.5 minutes and 5.5 minutes. The advantage of the 'cart' system is that you can physically hold, load and play a labelled cart, and stack it with others in the order you need them. How does it work? Simple. In the on-air situation, you put the required cartridge in the slot, open the correct fader and push the 'start' or 'five' button.

When the item has finished, the machine may stop ready to play again or fast forward to the stopping position. It is not 'cued'. Never try to take a cartridge out of a slot until it has stopped. Never stop a cartridge and remove it unless you mean to cue it up later. Leave it upside down to remind you. If the out cue or duration is incorrectly labelled on a commercial or promo, don't just swear and put it back in the rack, correct the label. One day you will be grateful someone else has done this for you.

With digital systems, you have to enter into the computer the number of the item and wait for it to be ready to play. For example, your commercial log in the studio will list, say, four adverts in the break as numbers 5438, 7865, 9674 and 3656. You tap these numbers into the keyboard of the digital storage system and assign each advert a 'channel' of the system, in the same way that you put a cart into a chosen slot. Systems vary, but pushing the play button usually turns the illuminated code number into a digital readout which counts down in seconds to the end of the advert. There is no need to know what the final word or out cue of the advert is, since when the countdown reaches zero, the advert is over. You can then play the next advert, or set up the system so that a spent channel can trigger the next one, and so on. Remember these systems are totally dependent on a hard disk; there are no tapes to rewind, and pushing 'play' will give instant sound. One day even the most low budget stations will enjoy technology like this.

Microphones

The main thing to watch out for is 'popping' – this is the explosion of sound created when speaking too close to the microphone capsule. My own voice is very prone to this, especially on the letter P. You can avoid this by putting acoustically transparent 'pop shields' on the capsule; speaking at a 45° angle to the microphone can also work wonders.

Remember you won't always hear pops on headphones, so record yourself saying plenty of Ps and play it back over loudspeakers with a decent bass response to check the best position. Too far away and you will sound lifeless and thin, too close and you will risk popping. A professional microphone usually gives the best results if your mouth is about three to four inches away from it.

Note that when you put the fader up on your microphone channel, the loudspeakers will cut out. This is to prevent feedback or howl-round. It's the reason why radio presenters have to wear headphones.

Get those flying hours in!

Just like aircraft pilots who have to log hours in the sky, any time you can clock up driving a radio desk is essential experience. Even a simple semi-professional affair at a hospital radio station will help you fully to understand the basics. During a self-operated radio show, working the gear must be second-nature to you. Just as experienced motorists can carry out an interesting conversation while safely driving the car, so you will learn to use all your active brainpower to put into those words coming out of your mouth, while your hands work the knobs automatically.

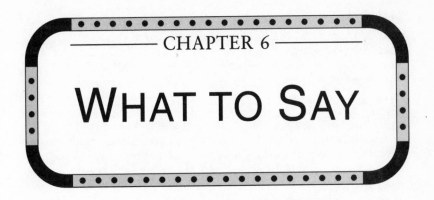

CHAPTER 6

WHAT TO SAY

*O*NCE THEY UNDERSTAND the studio equipment, surely anybody can string a few records together? However, it's not that simple. It's what you *say* (or don't say) in the 'links' between them that ensures whether you get (and keep) your job as a radio presenter.

All programme controllers have their own idea of what the content of a programme should be, but most experienced radio people agree that a successful daytime programme on an average music station should consist of a *mixture of types of links*. For example, a show full of information about records or concert news would be fine for a specialist jazz or soul show, but this style used on a mid-morning weekday show would be inappropriate for its listeners, who would find it hopelessly tedious.

To help you to achieve this variety in your show, this chapter breaks down the different types of radio links. (Your audition tape should include a good mix of these to show your versatility.) When you listen to the radio, see if you can identify the types.

The 'that was, this is' link

■ Gives pace and flow to your programme.
■ Links two songs which go well back-to-back.
■ Useful when it's a programme with little or no feature or personality content; for example, a chart show.

EXAMPLE

'A hot new song from Tempest, and "One to Wrong". It's four thirteen, and a classic from 1982 on the Z . . . 103.5, ZFM!'

TIPS

☑ Start the next song at full volume a split second before you speak, especially if it has a 'hard' start, then fade down to talk over the instrumental lead-in. This reinforces the impression of slick pace, and disciplines you into talking for only a few seconds, just as long as the talk-over time for the next song. ('Talk-over time' is the duration of any instrumental lead into the main vocals.)

☑ Try to include the station name somewhere in *every* type of link; it may be in a promo, a jingle, or you may say it. In this type of short link, the station name is reinforced if it is the *last* thing said.

☑ Think twice before announcing the names of really big hits. Doesn't everybody *know* you've just played Queen's 'Bohemian Rhapsody'?

☑ Unless you've been asked to do a show in this way, be aware that a radio programme consisting entirely of '*That was, this is*' links can be extremely tedious, unless there's some other element like a chart rundown.

The trail link

■ Teases listeners to keep listening.

■ Makes it sound as if lots of things are happening on your station.

■ Consists of anything that mentions future items, songs, features or programmes.

EXAMPLE

'Don't forget today we're giving you one more chance to win a ZFM Power Prize – Claire Mitchell of Short Green will be the first under the spotlight in the race to win £1,035! That's in about twenty minutes – stay tuned to your FM friend – ZFM on 103.5.'

TIPS

☑ Don't give too much information away, make it snappy yet clear.

☑ Be really enigmatic if you like – 'If you've got Edam cheese in your sandwiches today, you could end up in court – find out *why* in the next hour, here on ZFM!'

☑ When plugging colleagues' future programmes, check that the information in the studio trail book or on any memo you have is up-to-date. Why sound ignorant by getting it wrong?

☑ When trailing music to come in the next hour, don't be tempted to read endless lists of artists from the computer print-out. Mention three or four bands at most. Be wary of mentioning one-hit wonders; it will be obvious which song you're going to play.

☑ If the listener hears an artist who's had a string of hits, they'll hope you're going to play their favourite from that artist – *and will stay tuned to find out.*

The music and gig information link

■ Makes you sound informed about the music you're playing.
■ Makes the station sound upfront and 'in the know'.

EXAMPLE

'There it is, out at last as a single, just as we predicted, one of the finest tracks from the Shades of Time album – 'Love Dance' – with an extended mix of the CD version. Don't forget ZFM presents the band live at the Paramount Theatre next Thursday the 12th, and the tickets are selling fast – book your seats for a night of quality rock – from the Z – 103.5.'

TIPS

☑ Make use of press releases sent with new records. You can sometimes discover gems of information about artists or songs. If you use quotes from a music paper article, always say, briefly, which publication you are quoting from, as listeners may wish to read further.

☑ Mention release information about new records, but beware of making the link a blatant plug for record companies and their products.

☑ Always be proud if your station has a record release first. However, never admit 'we've put it on the playlist at last' or that 'Wazzock records have got round to sending us a copy at last'.

Never air your grievances about the internal politics of the playlist or release distribution. Listeners don't care.

The gag link

- Demonstrates that you're a wild and crazy guy / gal.
- Makes listeners react positively to your show (by laughing), reinforcing the bond between the listener and your station.
- The listener who likes your gag may tell others, thereby encouraging more people to tune in to your station. This is the 'shoutability' element: *anything* that gets people talking about your show and / or the radio station has to be a good thing.

EXAMPLE

'Am I tired this morning. I was up all night working on my new invention, a perpetual motion machine. It took me hours to get the stupid thing to *stop*.'

TIPS

- ☑ Only use jokes from a book or other source if you find them funny. Unless *you* understand the humour, the gag won't come over.
- ☑ Use gags which suit your personality and style. 'Hard-up-loser' stories will sound false if it's well known that you are rich and successful.
- ☑ Reword the gag and adapt it to suit your own personal style. Translate obviously American gags into English, if they work. I actually heard a local radio presenter in the UK tell a joke about the 'Gettysberg Address' that only visiting American tourists would understand.
- ☑ Never reveal that you're about to tell a gag. Obvious giveaways are introductions: *'Did you hear the one about . . .'* or *'My friend is so fat that . . .'*. Disguise the gag by making the subject of the joke relevant to the previous song or subject you're talking about. Don't laugh at your own jokes unless you're *really* sure it doesn't annoy the audience.
- ☑ Always ad-lib gags. Never read one out word-for-word as it will sound stilted and false, unless you're very experienced. However, always keep the *punchline* written down in front of you in case your mind suddenly goes blank!

☑ A mildly amusing punchline can sound dynamite if you:

(1) ...really believe in the gag. Think that it really *is* very funny, and you'll project this in the way you say it. Have confidence!

(2) ...practise timing. A pause before the punchline can work wonders.

(3) ...play anything with a loud start immediately after the punchline. This can be a jingle, advertisement or song. This will make your gag sound funnier than it really is.

(4) ...say nothing after the punchline. *Nothing!*

The observation link

■ Makes the presenter sound human and alert. Nothing is more boring than listening to someone who works in a vacuum, spouting endless cliché DJ links and irrelevant music facts.

■ Helps you relate to the listener, project your personality and paint a picture of your lifestyle in the real world.

EXAMPLE

The Eagles and 'Life in the Fast Lane' just for you if you're in your car. Maybe you're in the rush hour jam at a junction where once again *no one* is letting you in the queue! I know, everybody is pretending not to see you – they're looking straight ahead. Actually, *what* you drive determines who lets you in. Have you noticed that a Volkswagen will let you in if you drive a Volkswagen? Peugeots let in Peugeots and so on. So if you're in a T-junction jam right now, driving a rare 1958 soft-top Morgan . . . you're really stuffed.

TIPS

☑ Never write out any link word-for-word – you won't sound spontaneous. Put key words down, and remember the rest!

☑ Don't ramble, and make sure there is a punchline – either a comic gag or a strong point at the end.

The anecdote link

■ Like an observation link, makes the DJ into a broadcaster, making him or her *relate* to the listener. Anecdotes told well tell the listener more about you; and help you to build a following.

EXAMPLE

'I had a pile of letters at home yesterday, most of it junk mail. Why send it to me? Doesn't their computerised mailing list database tell them I'm *not* the type of man who needs a shelf-full of their encyclopaedias or a timeshare on the Algarve? Actually, yesterday I also got an invoice from my local furniture shop along with a note saying it was one year old. I sent it back along with a birthday card.'

TIP

☑ Obviously you can make up anecdotes, but they'll sound more believable if they really happened to you. Even stupid things can make great links. Maybe today you locked your car keys in your car or a chain store assistant actually said 'Good morning' to you. (No, that would be too incredible to believe.)

The current affairs comment link

■ Further relates to the listener and the events in his or her world.
■ Sounds as though you care about things, and are not wrapped up in the cosy world of music and showbusiness.

EXAMPLE

'With all the recent gloom over the trade figures, it was good to see at that press conference yesterday that one UK business has had a dramatic increase over the year. In fact, we British are getting better every year, yes, of course, I'm talking about *crime* – I wonder when they're going to privatise it?'

TIPS

☑ Make sure you understand the facts before you comment.
☑ Keep your comments inoffensive, and don't slander anyone.
☑ If in doubt about the latter, always quote the source – 'The *Daily Bugle* must really be in trouble after calling Dr Luigi "a raving queen". . .', etc.
☑ Don't waffle and make sure there is a punchline. Remember, a punchline in radio doesn't have to be funny – just be sure that the point you are making has a definite and strong ending.

The travel information link
....

■ Relates to the area.
■ Provides a service to the listener.
■ Makes the station sound as if it knows what is going on.

EXAMPLE

'ZFM Travel News. We have problems on the A602 through Borrington again this morning; please avoid the stretch of road approaching the roadworks into Lea Green. The diversions are well signposted and will take you through . . .'

TIPS

☑ Don't bore regular listeners by repeating the same things every day. If any important roadworks go on for a long time, think of different words to use each day while the facts stay the same.

☑ Don't gabble – keep road names and numbers clear. If no one can understand what you're saying, why bother? If you use a music 'bed' or sound effects track under your voice, keep it low.

☑ Remember that radio is one-to-one. Avoid pluralisms: never say, 'motorists' or, 'if you are *all* in your cars'. Say 'If *you* are driving . . .'

The weather link
....

■ Provides a service to the listener.
■ Makes the station sound informed.

EXAMPLE

'A wet start to the day, but the rain will clear by noon and we'll have a dry afternoon. Today's maximum temperature, 11 degrees Celsius, that's 52 degrees Fahrenheit. Currently it's 8 degrees Celsius, measured at Bosley Tower, Mopchester, and at ZFM!'

TIPS

☑ Never 'throw away' weather. Many listeners may genuinely want to know what the weather will be, so don't race through or slur the words, no matter how boring you think it is.

☑ Try to look out of the window before reading the weather. Forecasts are often wrong – update your information if necessary.

☑ If the forecast you have *is* wrong, never say: 'My weather says it *should* be sunny but it's teeming down outside! What a load of rubbish!' The listener ought to have the impression that your station is the fount of all knowledge. Why admit that you take the forecast from the fax machine or from Teletext?

☑ A good scam to make your station sound as if it covers a larger area than it does is to pretend that you have weather stations at places in the outer fringe area. A Southampton station would say, for example: 'In Salisbury it's sunny now . . .' or whatever. Alternate fringe towns at every read.

The community noticeboard / 'What's on' link

▪ Relates your station to the area it serves.
▪ Provides a service to the listener.
▪ Gives the impression you'll broadcast information the listener sends in.

EXAMPLE

'You'll find some fabric bargains and help raise cash for a charity this afternoon at Wallington Town Hall from 2 pm. There will be quality fabrics of all sorts on sale at vastly reduced prices. All profits will go to Wateraid. That's the big Material Bargain Show at the Town Hall this afternoon from 2 pm.'

TIPS

☑ 'What's ons' can be very boring – keep them short and clear. However, always repeat the location and time for half-asleep punters.

☑ Charity plugs are fine, but don't upset your sales department by giving a free plug to commercial ventures. They are trying to make business owners *pay* for their mentions!

☑ Be wary of reading from old press releases or leaflets. Check that the event or gig hasn't been cancelled.

The newspaper / magazine link

■ Relates to listeners who have seen the same article or story.
■ Keeps a current affairs element alive.
■ Adds interest to your show.

EXAMPLE

'I see from this morning's *Telegraph* that the controversial research institute for chemical and biological warfare, the infamous Porton Down, is going to be renamed. Always the same, isn't it? If some sensitive unit gets a bad reputation, the name magically changes overnight as if the previous place never existed. Remember the nuclear plant, Windscale, that became Sellafield? I bet they're busy choosing a new name for Porton Down now – Happy Bunny Valley.'

TIPS

☑ Remember the laws of slander and contempt of court – if you don't know exactly what these are, find out. It's well worth investing in a copy of *McNae's Essential Law for Journalists* (Butterworths) – the broadcasting industry's bible on all matters legal. Also, unless the Programme Controller says so, do not be politically biased. Instead of criticising, say, specific government departments, use the more general 'they' – representing the large grey establishment.

☑ Always credit the publication if you're using an 'Exclusive'. Listeners can then buy it if they want to follow up, and the publisher is kept away from the telephone to his solicitor; after all your radio station hasn't bought the rights to broadcast this exclusive news.

☑ If you don't have to credit the paper or magazine, disguise it as an Observation Link. In other words, make it sound as if you know about the story already and are commenting off the top of your head. Why sound as if you're just reading from the paper? *Sound informed.* Try and tie it in with the subject matter or title of the previous song to make it sound natural.

☑ Again, always have a punchline, even if it's not funny. There must be a final point to your reading the story. If you have to resort to 'Well, ha ha, there you go . . .' or, 'Er, one of the stories in today's papers, folks . . .', you have failed.

☑ *Think* before you read. Is the item genuinely interesting, funny or relevant? Do your listeners *really* want to know about yet another tabloid sex survey?

The event-relevant link

- Takes advantage of the immediacy of radio.
- Ties in on-air features to the event – for example, a regular cookery slot might feature making parkin for bonfire night.
- Includes virtually any type of link which talks about a time, event or season.

EXAMPLE

'With the school summer holidays coming up in two weeks, we thought it was about time we found out what activities were on offer in our area . . .'

'This Maundy Thursday business is a great farce. As soon as the old people receive the Maundy money from the Queen, they're in a cab round to the nearest coin collector's shop as fast as they can say "Thank you, Ma'am".'

TIPS

☑ Don't forget to link in local events as well as national ones. A local motor show, royal visit or official opening of a new office block are all valid events to tie in to a creative radio link.

☑ Remember the diversity of people's tastes and interests. Don't assume that in the summer everyone is going to have a barbecue at the weekend, or that in the winter they are going to the big match. Don't worry that you may be relating to smaller groups of people. When you read dedications you are almost certainly relating to even fewer.

The local interest link

- Directly involves the listeners and has relevance to their lives.
- Makes the station sound as though it cares about the community in its transmission area.

EXAMPLE

(The local story: Developers building a huge office block in the shape of a pyramid in Stockport go bust before completion. Legal wrangles leave it still unfinished over a year later. Another developer completes the building, but it's still empty. A big white elephant, the whole town knows about it.)

'With April the first round the corner, all of us here are trying to conjure up a great April Fool's spoof. What shall we come up with this year? UFOs over Altrincham? Shall we claim that they've trained the Tatton Park deer to talk? Could we say that they've sold the office space at that pyramid on the Brinksway? No, no, *no one* would ever believe that!'

TIP

☑ Try and cover as much ground as possible; you can combine local-interest, event-relevant and gag links all in one.

The competition link

■ Competitions encourage greedy punters to satisfy their materialistic urges!
■ Non-participating listeners usually enjoy the vicarious winning or losing experience.
■ Competitions encourage listeners to get involved with the station.
■ Competitions can be tied in with a spot advertising campaign. Clients might even provide the prizes.

TIPS

☑ Never say a competition is simple. Why insult your listeners' intelligence? Your competition may be like a two-piece jigsaw for anyone with above-average intelligence, but don't say so on air. Your listeners will feel fools if they get it wrong, and why should they bother to enter anyway if it is 'so simple'?
☑ Never admit that your write-in competition has had little response. If there is a real disaster for whatever reason, make up winners' names and addresses. Pick fairly well-known names and long streets!
☑ On a phone-in competition, don't give any clues to the answers, unless it's a 'just for fun' game. Also, never give competitors more than the allotted time to answer. It's unfair, and devalues the whole competition.

The dedication / request link

The reason radio stations do requests and dedications is not just so that listeners can hear their names on the radio; a good proportion must miss their mentions anyway. Dedications:

■ Make the station sound accessible to the public.

■ Give the impression that the listeners are enjoying, even *choosing*, the music the station is playing.

■ Mention names and places that people will relate to – important if your selling point is your locality.

TIPS

☑ Always say the recipient's name twice. Make it clear who the mention is for.

☑ Always give full name and area. If all you've got is Mr Smith, and a smudged postmark, bin it.

☑ Never say, 'Sorry, we haven't got that record,' or 'We're not going to play that rubbish you've asked for.' Simply don't mention the fact that a specific record has been asked for which you are not going to play.

☑ Always read through the letter first. Circle in a red pen the facts you will use in your link.

☑ Never make fun of people's names . . . *ever*. Make sure you pronounce them correctly too.

☑ Never read out the number of the house, for security reasons. Road and area is fine.

The pre-recorded insert link

■ Adds originality to your programme.

■ Gives an extra dimension to a continuous music programme.

■ Stretches your imagination, and shows the boss how clever you can be in the production studio.

EXAMPLES

(1) Pre-recorded sketches with comic characters who happen to barge into your studio.

(2) Self-contained comedy or drama serials that you can link into.

(3) Edited vox pops in which you have asked the listeners their views on a subject, maybe mixed with a music track or 'bed' to give pace.

TIPS

☑ Liaise with your Programme Controller so that you know exactly how far you can go with regard to duration, budget, taste and decency.

☑ Have a good ten or so in the can so that brilliant sketches can be interspersed with ones which didn't turn out so well.
☑ Don't be afraid to repeat the insert at a later part of your show, when audience surveys show that a substantial number of different people are listening.

The live guest link

■ Adds a point of interest to your show.
■ Shows your skills as an interviewer.

TIPS

☑ Many guests are only on the radio circuit to plug their latest book. Get information out of the author, not just a series of references to the book. Ensure you make the interview interesting in its own right.
☑ If the guest is good, split up the chat with records; interested listeners will stay tuned for longer, uninterested listeners won't get bored.
☑ Don't be overwhelmed by famous guests – it is your programme and not theirs.

You may feel that I have gone into too much detail here, but if you want to get a presenter's job on radio, you'll have to know how to handle all these links, no matter what type of programme you're aiming at. A lot of my tips may be self-evident, and certain maverick programme controllers may tell you to do the opposite. They're the boss, so fine. The bottom line that we all agree on, however, is:

You must always give the listener a reason for listening

People rarely tune in out of blind loyalty to a radio station. There is a huge choice for the listener these days. You must offer something that is lacking in the other shows being broadcast at the same time. When you get your break on the air, set up a meeting with the programme controller and decide on your strong points, and weave together a structure of a killer show that you hope will make the opposition switch off its transmitter and go home.

Radio presenters are not 'DJs'

Please, don't 'turn into a DJ' as soon as the microphone is on. The listener wants to hear *you*, the person, not some inane personage who says the sorts of things he *thinks* radio people should say. Real people in the real world don't, for example, get on to a bus, wave their arms about and scream:

> *'Hey, well, there you go, bus driver, just coming up to the hour of 11, right on time for the start of the week, eh? How about giving me a ticket to the big city where it all happens 24 hours a day, all the time, non-stop? Wow! Power to your wheels, dude. Have a great day, won't you, on this legendary 12A bus route – anyone you'd like to say hello to?'*

You are communicating to real people, so why not speak their language? I'm always amused to hear these people prattle on at a hundred miles an hour when they're broadcasting on their own, then as soon as they have a guest interview they are forced to turn into a normal human being again. After all, it's impossible to interview people sensibly if you're a cliché DJ.

How to spot a 'cliché DJ'

■ He talks out of the side of his mouth in a slurred, affected manner, at an abnormal speed or in a hyper-animated way. I say 'He' because this affliction is rarely suffered by female presenters.

■ He is so obsessed with 'tight radio' that when he runs out of sensible things to say halfway through an introduction of a song he'll pad with any old rubbish to fill up to the vocal start, maybe even singing or whistling over the record.

■ He's obviously insincere. For example, he'll chat to phone-in contestants he's never met and call them 'mate' and laugh uncontrollably at the listeners' remarks for no reason whatsoever.

■ He states the obvious or repeats what has already been said. For example, after the jingle which says 'ZFM *Competition Time*', he'll immediately bawl, '*Yesh, indeed! It's* ZFM *competition Time . . .!*' Tautology? You can say that again.

■ He shouts to the next presenter just coming into the studio, '*Hey, Damian . . . LOVE the tie!*' The other presenter mumbles something hopelessly off-mic so only the cliché DJ, who then dissolves into nervous giggles, hears it.

- He habitually uses certain meaningless words like 'great', 'brilliant', 'there you go', 'you know', and so on.
- The most intelligent observation on the show is about the state of the radio station coffee.
- He mentions his name at virtually every link.
- He announces: 'It's Monday, July the 3rd 1995.' Why say the year? Is it for the benefit of time travellers who may be tuning in on the way to the H.G. Wells convention?

Maybe you recognise a few of these awful traits in your own presentation demos or programmes. None of us is perfect. But remember: Don't be someone you're not; relax and be yourself, listeners will relate to you better. Playing yourself is easiest. If you want to make it into television, ask yourself: how many TV presenters do you know who sound like DJs? QED.

CHAPTER 7
THE RADIO PHONE-IN

IF YOU'RE LOOKING for an entry into broadcasting, but feel that you haven't the empathy with modern music to become a radio music show presenter, or haven't the formal journalistic background to make it into a newsroom, how about hosting a radio phone-in? You'll need a broad knowledge of current affairs – and local affairs as well, for local radio. You will have an opinion on virtually everything and the ability to talk your way out of trouble.

Previous jobs of local radio phone-in hosts round the country vary from newspaper column writers to club comedians. Recording an audio showtape would not be appropriate as part of an application; creating a 'name' for yourself in other circles would be. You could get yourself involved in local organisations; you could even become a councillor or a magistrate. The important thing is to know as much as you can about the needs and character of your region. When you've done all that, why not invite your local radio station boss out to lunch and impress him or her with your gift of the gab! A programme controller's ideal phone-in host is someone who has a passion for the area his station serves, who understands the identity of the people who live there, and who has the intelligence to discuss virtually any subject with authority.

Sony Award-winning Northerner Allan Beswick is a good example of the enquiring personality with a broad background who makes a successful phone-in host. He worked as an electronic engineer, a junior audit clerk, a psychiatric nurse and had five years in the army before joining the Citizens' Advice Bureau.

Radio City in Liverpool saw Allan's potential when he was invited into the studio to provide the listeners with consumer advice. He was given his own para-legal advice programme, the success of which led to phone-ins on BBC Radio Blackburn (now BBC Radio Lancashire),

Metro Radio in Newcastle and Red Rose in Preston. Here the audience ratings for his late-night programme broke all records, and the listenership at midnight was greater than at midday: a previously unheard-of situation. His success as a no-nonsense phone-in host and interviewer now continues on BBC GMR.

Allan has this advice for would-be phone-in presenters: 'You have got to be well informed, otherwise you are likely to fall flat on your face if a caller brings up a subject you are not clued up on. I've got the sort of mind which is naturally agile and enquiring and am forever taking in and storing information. At home, I take five daily newspapers and subscribe to a dozen magazines from the *Economist* to *Private Eye*. It's almost an obsession to be up to date with what is happening in the world and to whom. My advice is that if you have to force yourself to read the papers or remind yourself to listen to the news every hour, then you're not the right person for the job. You have to be genuinely interested in people and events. My on-air personality is perceived to be arrogant, stubborn and even rude, but I actually very rarely give my opinions on-air. My job is to be a "Mr Nosey" – to explore every facet of a caller's viewpoint. I find that if I slap them around a bit, it makes for a better and ultimately more satisfying conversation.'

Phone-ins usually take one of the following three formats:

■ You have a live guest who answers questions from listeners after an initial interview.

■ You start the programme with a whole list of stories in the news that people might want to call in about. It is important to do this right and bring up possible areas of lively discussion, or you won't get the calls.

■ You don't have any menu and leave the subjects to the listeners. This format will usually only work on well-established shows.

Presenters should have phone-in staff or at least a producer in a separate room who will do all the setting up for you. Unless you have records on your show, you will never do it all on your own. How will you answer the phones when you're talking to someone on the air?

Your backroom helpers will answer calls and establish what subject listeners want to talk about, taking their names and telephone numbers. They will then call them back *'if the producer can fit you in'*, in other words, if their points are worthy of airtime.

In the studio, you will be handed pieces of paper with messages like: 'Mary, line 6, divorce laws'. Or this information may be displayed on a VDU monitor in front of you. Somehow, out of this stream of disparate callers you have to make an interesting and informative programme with hardly a break for a sip of your coffee.

Obscenities on air

The Radio Authority insists that all phone-in programmes have a delay system to prevent swear words or slander from reaching the airwaves. Your station may have an analogue machine, which is simply a tape-recorder with a replay head seven seconds back from the record head, or a digital version which senses slight gaps in the output and 'stretches' them until what the listener hears is seven seconds behind the output of the studio.

Given this time-delay, you would obviously be monitoring *studio* output in your headphones, and not off-air output unless you really want a headache. Here's what happens.

YOU: *'On line 4 is Dave Filth from Dunstable. What's your view?'*
DAVE: *'Well, I think we should tell the jugheads to **** off!'*

Immediately, you pull Dave's fader down to the end-stop and flick your monitor switch from listening to *studio* output to *off-air*. You will, amazingly, hear life as it was seven seconds ago. Time travel is possible in radio. You will hear yourself say, '*On line 4 is Dave Filth from Dunstable. What's your view?*'

After the word 'view', you push the DUMP button on the delay machine, which switches the transmitter back to taking the direct *live* output from your desk. At the same time, you could push the start button of a cartridge carrying the sound effect of a telephone being slammed down and the resulting tone. Alternatively, you say, 'Dave? Dave? Are you there, Dave? No, we seem to have lost Dave from Dunstable. On Line 5 we have . . .' And so on. Dave sits at home thinking he's shocked the world, and the rest of the listeners are none the wiser. You then push the STRETCH button during the next call to get back to your seven seconds' delay.

Controversial phone-ins

Sometimes the delay machine is deliberately not used. (*'Sorry, Radio Authority, the engineers were working on it that night.'*) A bit of controversy on the radio always stirs up the press and the presenter is usually in the clear as long as it is obvious that they were not encouraging any form of slanderous or obscene comments. Playing devil's advocate always whips up a few lively calls and it is up to you, the presenter, to try to get a balance between the participants.

Before you start to host a phone-in, you must decide what type of presenter you want to be. Do you want to be a neutral diplomat pitting caller against caller, or do you want to get involved and have arguments with your callers?

If you choose the latter, be sure you won't be losing more listeners than you'll gain.

Phone-in tips

☑ Have a list of experts in a book or electronic organiser next to you. If you talk to a listener who has a grievance about a local firm, a bank or the council, you can then advise them, with a certain amount of authority, who to call. With luck, you will give the impression these people are your personal mates, all thanks to a little hard work sourcing contacts before the series.

☑ If you are worried that no one will call in, find a few people with controversial views on the subject before doing the programme, and call them at the start of the show. Make it sound as if they have rung you; this will usually stimulate plenty of calls.

☑ On local radio, include a good mixture of local and world issues to maintain interest throughout the programme.

☑ Don't be afraid to cut callers short if you are getting bored with their comments. If *you* are getting bored, you can bet the listener is as well.

☑ Keep a list of previous callers who are intelligent, articulate talkers. People who tend to have a view on everything are invaluable to call on days when, for some reason, no one is ringing in.

☒ Never read listeners' telephone numbers on air, even if they say it's OK. Ask people to call in to be given them. A pervert or heavy breather may want to use the number for their obscene fantasies; they will be put off if they have to call the station first.

Hosting a radio phone-in can be stimulating work and a good presenter in this traditionally late-night slot can be the kingpin of the whole station's success. The downside is a twilight existence, and sleep doesn't come easily at two in the morning when, although the shift is finished, your head is still buzzing with the worries of countless listeners.

CHAPTER 8

THE BREAK INTO TV

HOW DO YOU GET into presentation work on television? Gatecrash the right parties? Bribe producers? Sell your soul?

The first thing to remember is that a TV station is not a forbidden planet and you don't need written permission just to walk into reception. Forget any glamorous image and imagine it to be what it is . . . a place of work. If you can do a job that needs to be done, they'll pay you for it; it's as simple as that. The hardest thing is to get your first break, which you'll achieve through a knowledge of the jobs around, through the effective communication of your talent to the right people, and through persistence, ingenuity, and a bit of luck.

Presenters' jobs are advertised rarely, and then often only as a sop to management to prove there's nobody better than the producer's original choice. Sometimes a TV station has a stable of presenters who are assigned jobs in the news and various regional shows by a head of department. If this is the case, you will have to discover, through your dealings, who actually hires and fires talent. Producers may have their hands tied here when it comes to choosing presenters.

If the programme makers have free rein, it's open season, so go for it. Find out their names, and suggest new features. Don't criticise their existing presenters, but mention how your unique style could add an extra dimension to the show. Badger, but don't pester. Explain your ideas, but don't ramble. The average producer is a tormented individual who has to juggle many balls in the air. Your letters will go straight in the bin unless you can show you've got something to offer.

When there's news in the air that a programme is looking for presenters, the producer is suddenly snowed under with tapes and CVs, usually from faceless agents. That's why your taking a personal, individual approach is much more likely to bear fruit than your staying at home and hoping an agent will do all the work for you. In any case, agents will only take you on if you've a decent track record behind you, or if you can prove you really are very special.

There is no magic formula that will help you achieve your first break in TV. There are as many different experiences as there are presenters, but in every case it all boils down to having talent, ability and that vital, elusive factor: luck.

Annie McKie is a co-presenter of the BBC TV regional news programme from Bristol, *News West*. Her break came from a case of mistaken identity. 'I always wanted to be a performer. After graduating from drama school in London, life on stage as an actress was very exciting but also very uncertain.' Annie put herself on the market as a corporate video presenter using her real name, Annie Rice. 'One of the clients booked me thinking I was *Anneka* Rice – and on the day wondered where the long blonde hair and jumpsuit was! In the end I presented the video to everyone's satisfaction and was given more and more work.'

Annie used extracts of her corporate video work to compile a showtape which eventually led to work as a newsreader and presenter for BBC TV's regional programmes for the West Country. She also hosts radio programmes for the BBC and this is where she feels potential TV presenters can most effectively learn their basic skills. 'My advice to newcomers is to get any job in radio, do it very, very well – never complain – come up with ideas of your own and somehow make yourself indispensable. You have got to offer more than you're asked to do. Radio teaches you about getting the voice right, timing, editing and editorial skills which of course all apply in television work too. Above all, never be complacent – you've got to stay one step ahead of everyone else. Keep your eyes and ears open so you will be in the best possible position to take advantage of any opportunities which come your way.'

At twenty-six, Toby Anstis is well established at BBC TV as one of the main faces of children's programming. 'I knew I wanted to go into television when I was at school but I came up against a barrage of negativity. I started doing hospital radio when I was fourteen and got the bug – for me, presenting is all about sharing ideas and things that interest you with other people. I did a degree in Marketing and Psychology and started working in a marketing job in London during the week while doing some presenting on a local cable radio network at the weekends.

'My big break came when I put a show reel together while working at the cable station and sent it to the BBC. They said they would see me so I went in and within two hours they had offered me a six-month contract.

'Because of my youth, children's broadcasting seemed a natural area to go into. Let's face it – when you really want to broadcast you can't do much else if you're only twenty-two.' In the world of TV, Toby is right. Apart from the young VJs on MTV's satellite service, most programmes need presenters with more experience of life. This is why so many young people start their broadcasting careers on radio, where a lack of age can be disguised with a resonant voice.

One of Toby's colleagues, Sally Gray, tells me how she got her first break: 'I studied Media Studies at Edinburgh and it has always been children's television which has interested me. There were no openings in the BBC children's department at the time I graduated, but I was lucky enough to get a job as a secretary in the "reserve" which meant I was able to work on a whole variety of programmes, such as *Question Time*. Whoever I came across in the different departments, I made sure they knew how much I wanted to become a presenter and people started to give me lots of advice. I met this girl in the corridor and we got chatting. She said she was going to be a PA on a new children's show. "Who's presenting it?" I asked. "They haven't decided yet," she said. Well that was it. For the next few days I left endless messages on the producer's answer machine, I wrote letters to him and eventually he called me back and said he'd see me. He gave me the job and I spent the next three months working on the show in Edinburgh!'

Sally suggests that you should sell yourself to as many people as possible. 'Send your show reel to everyone – to the addresses in the back of *Broadcast* magazine, everywhere. Don't bother with presenter courses or professional show reels – just go out with a good friend and a video camera and do it. Do it at the dentist's, in the street – just do it. Toby Anstis did his show reel by getting his mate to record him changing his flat tyre!'

Although Sally did not take advantage of training courses, I would suggest that you don't dismiss them straight away. My advice would be to check them out before signing up for anything: talk to previous students, ask about your tutor's experience. Anybody can set themselves up with a video camera and an edit suite and call themselves a presenter's training school. There are many excellent organisations around, but even these may not be suitable for your particular needs. Join a training course only if you're completely satisfied that the time and money you will spend will be worthwhile. If you are creative and technically able, your cash might be better spent producing showtapes yourself.

Both Toby and Sally were lucky that their ambitions to work in TV were realised very quickly. Of course, many presenters have a grounding in radio before they find an opportunity in TV. I am loath to use the phrase 'stepping stone' because this implies that radio is in some way inferior to television. The appeal of being in-vision and the increased salary heighten the glamour of TV, but radio is often more enjoyable to work in. Radio has more opportunities for newcomers than TV simply because radio stations usually have less money and have to produce up to twenty-four hours' worth of original live programming for their area each day. So radio programme controllers are more likely to test out new presenters in the off-peak hours where skills can be honed, and where the horror of making an on-air mistake won't be visually apparent. It is also very rare for a new face to be launched straight onto network TV. The ITV and BBC regions – traditional home of the first break in television – have limited hours of regional programming.

Beverley Ashworth is a freelance broadcaster based in the North of England. Her work is split between in-vision continuity / newsreading and corporate video presentation. She also has regular radio programmes on the north-west regional jazz and blues station, JFM 100.4. 'My talent for broadcasting was discovered after a joke misfired,' she says. 'After working at a few advertising agencies and a video production company, I was involved with organising the auditions for a team of continuity presenters for the new Central TV East region. We recorded test tapes with a huge number of applicants and, to put it politely, we saw some sights! At the end I was persuaded into performing what was meant to be a spoof – but when the Head of Presentation saw the tape, he invited me to Nottingham for a studio audition. I made it to the final 20!'

Beverley actually ended up as an in-vision presenter at Granada TV in Manchester. She has these words of advice for newcomers: 'It all comes down to cool professionalism, enthusiasm and, in the case of my job, being able to adapt what you are doing at a moment's notice. Appearing on TV changes some people into selfish prima donnas, who don't seem to realise how privileged they are. After all, a situation in which you are paid extremely well for more or less being yourself is very enviable.

'I am very lucky in that I can combine writing, television, radio and corporate work – but I don't take any of it for granted. I was given some excellent advice very early on: *Treat everyone how you would like to be treated – and remember, whoever you meet on the way up will usually still be there on the way down!*'

The 'hassle factor' of a television show can be enormous. There can be a lot of hanging around on filming days, and your items or even entire programmes can be dropped from air at very short notice.

Nevertheless, TV has many attractions. In the next chapter I cover the TV presenter's job in detail. But if a presenter's job seems out of your league at the moment, let's look at other job opportunities which might prove helpful to start your career on the inside.

Continuity announcing

If you want to present on television, the idea of introducing the programmes may seem extremely attractive. However, if you really want to end up fronting a variety of shows or get into news reporting, be aware that the continuity announcers' department is usually completely separate from programming. The announcer sits with a camera and/or microphone in front of him or her in a soundproofed box usually overlooking the TV station's master presentation console.

This is where all the programmes from different sources are routed to air with any animated logos, promotion trails, and commercials. You wouldn't have anything to do with this routing, the Transmission Controller (in ITV) or Presentation Manager (at the BBC) would do all that, but your job would be to introduce (or 'trail') programmes at set junctions throughout your shift. All BBC continuity is voice-over only, but many ITV stations have various points during the shifts where you appear in vision. Regional newsreading might be required of you here, too.

PLUS POINTS
- The pay is usually very good.
- Rosters are usually worked out weeks in advance so you can plan your life.
- There's a certain thrill in not knowing if a breakdown is just round the corner, so your ad-libbing skills can come to the fore.

MINUS POINTS
- You may have to endure the frustration of having to read other people's scripts, when you feel you could write better yourself.
- Do you really want to sit in a box for ten hours at a time, looking at programmes you wouldn't consider enduring at home?

Programme researcher

The researcher can make the difference between an indifferent or brilliant programme. Most researchers who join the BBC or ITV companies have good degrees; but independent producers don't generally automatically reject non-degree-holders. Good ideas, intelligence, initiative and enthusiasm are the main things you'll need to do the job.

A researcher's job is to work closely with the producer, and sometimes the director as well, in finding people and locations, researching facts, collating library material: virtually all the components that will make the finished programme. You may be expected to write scripts and even direct your own items. You may be assigned to a documentary series with a different subject every week. You won't need to be an expert on say, theme parks, security devices, accounting frauds, terrorism or cancer, but you'll need to know *where* to get information from and *where* to find the people who can help you further. If you have intelligence and a ton of common sense, you'll do fine.

A researcher's job will get easier as your contact book gets fatter with the names of experts you've found on every subject under the sun.

PLUS POINTS
■ It's very rewarding to come up with the goods on schedule.
■ There will be plenty of opportunities to impress producers face-to-face and to show you're future on-screen reporter material.

MINUS POINTS
■ You'll spend a lot of time on the phone and visiting locations, and much of the work will lead to dead ends.
■ Long hours are expected of you, and deadlines can be very tight.

News camera operator

You may be attracted to the idea of being a camera operator on a TV news crew. You'll need operational, coordinational and artistic skills, as well as huge amounts of stamina and patience. You may drive long distances under impossible deadlines and then film half an hour's worth of shots in the pouring rain before being told that the story is being dropped. You'll be torn between creative picture-making and rushing to get the tape back to base in time. Camera operators usually cut their teeth as assistants: humping tripods, loading film, marking up video cassettes etc, and generally learning the art of news-gathering. Formal qualifications are not important; being able to prove you can do the job will keep you employed.

PLUS POINTS
■ You'll see all of life through your viewfinder, and you can learn tips off the professional presenters and reporters you work with.

- The pay can be excellent, and good camera operators are always asked back.

MINUS POINTS

- Unless you are lucky enough to get a staff job, as a freelance you will have to buy your own equipment: around £30,000 for a camera.
- You'll have to endure long hours and sometimes dangerous conditions.

Sound recordist

'In television, people think about pictures. They only worry about the sound if it's not there.' If I had a pound for every time I've heard that from a sound person . . . This complaint can be justified, however. The director in the studio gallery or out on the road just expects the sound to *be there*; the vision is what he or she is paid to worry about. Job satisfaction goes into a steep decline when the location director says a take was OK, even when you protest that an actor had knocked his radio microphone or an aircraft was clearly audible in a scene set in Victorian times . . . Again formal qualifications don't really matter; employers are not looking for a Tonmeister degree. A background in a recording studio or radio station will put you in a good position.

PLUS POINTS

- If you've a solid technical radio background, where you have 'driven' your own equipment, you should enjoy the work as a TV sound person.
- It can be challenging to determine where to place microphones, especially in a drama when they should not be seen.

MINUS POINT

- It's true that sound is only noticed when there's something wrong.

Video or film editor

This person's job is to transform all the video or film shot on location (the 'rushes') into the finished feature, commercial or programme. This is done by putting all the best 'takes' in the right order and, in the case of video editing, enhancing the footage with video effects or graphic inserts.

It's a quasi-technical/artistic job where the job satisfaction varies according to the director or reporter you're working for. Sometimes your artistic ability and creativity is drawn upon throughout the edit, and other times you just sit there merely cutting film or pushing buttons to order. Some media training courses offer you the opportunity to specialise in editing. However, many of today's top editors have picked it up as they went along.

PLUS POINTS

■ If you've an eye for a picture, you'll enjoy work satisfaction and decent pay.
■ A good video or film editor can really make indifferent shots come to life.

MINUS POINT

■ It's very unhealthy being hunched over equipment, staring at flickering screens.

Graphics designer

This is another artistic job that needs a good understanding of the technical side of broadcasting. When I started in TV, captions were made by rubdown letters on card that were simply placed in front of the camera. These days, everything is electronically generated for speed and flexibility. You may have boring days, typing and storing endless name captions for a documentary, but on other days enjoy putting together a fast-moving title sequence using all the latest electronic gadgets your budget will allow.

PLUS POINTS

■ If you're artistic with a good portfolio, and you're not technophobic, you may really enjoy the work.
■ The pay can be very good, although competition is fierce. A design subject studied to at least degree-standard is a must.

MINUS POINT

■ Graphics departments are not usually associated with programming ones, so you may feel left out of the team.

Press office / Public relations

A job in this department of a TV station would put you in a good position to angle for any production or presentation work, simply because you'd know what new programmes are being planned, and who is responsible for them. Your job would involve promoting new programmes and personalities, as well as organising functions which create a higher profile for the TV station. You may be responsible for writing information for listings magazines and organising audiences for studio programmes.

PLUS POINTS

■ Producers need you to sell their shows to the outside world. There will be plenty of opportunities to find out from them where new presentation talent is needed.

■ It can be very interesting learning about the background behind the shows and meeting established presenters and actors.

MINUS POINTS

■ Your office may be a long way from where the 'action' is going on.
■ Typing press releases all day can be a chore.

So what if none of the above suits your qualifications or abilities? If you know you'd be an A1 front person for a television show, it's important to meet and work with production staff who may hire and fire. What about the option of offering your services for free? Whereas radio stations need to take on keen, cheap or free workers to help on phone-ins, outside broadcasts, or general studio work, until fairly recently, their rich cousins at the TV stations didn't really need to do this. Television used to have the luxury of enough staff to do all the jobs twice over.

Things have changed. Many non-essential people have been made redundant to make ITV companies and BBC TV more lean and competitive. The iron grip of the unions is no longer there, and staff now have to do three or four jobs whereas before they could only do one. More and more programmes will be made by outside production companies and not by TV stations themselves. More companies making programmes means more opportunities to get in, since there will be more bosses to decide whether they like you or not. Hard times all around mean that people will be more receptive to enthusiastic people willing to help in research, secretarial work, floor managing or simply looking after studio guests. You may get little or no pay at first, but it's the experience you need, and the contacts you *have* to make, face-to-face. You must convince producers that you are a responsible, professional person who does not mind answering phones, stuffing fact-pack envelopes or filing viewers' letters for a short while. It's a two-way deal: you help their programme out in return for some weeks on the inside.

So how do you get this sort of work? Have a look in the *Contacts* Factfile at the end of this book. Make a list of the stations you'd be prepared to work at. I have listed the names (correct at time of publication) of the people you need to contact in each case. Normally the Head of Local Programmes or the Editor of the regional news magazine will be most receptive to enthusiastic, talented outsiders. Don't forget to contact programme producers direct, too. However, one problem here is that calling a producer whose name you have just read off an on-screen caption will usually result in your being told that the show was made months ago, and the team has now disbanded! Do some detective work and find out what shows are being made now, or what programme teams are about to be put together. The TV station press office should know what is happening. Pretend to be putting together a student magazine article if you're embarrassed to tell the truth. Even the switchboard operator or receptionist may be able to tell you those vital producers' names. Don't forget that many shows are made by independent producers at other locations.

You may think that there is a long list of enthusiastic outsiders calling up programmes daily, but in my experience it's simply not true. There are a lot of harassed producers out there trying to run busy but understaffed production offices who may be very grateful for your help for a short while. Write or phone but above all . . . impress. Your mission is to get inside the building, make contacts, get to know the way the station or production company works, read noticeboards and get a small but important foothold in television.

If you are at the stage where you cannot afford to offer your services free, then you can still get a feel of TV, and visit places where you might have the opportunity to meet production staff. Get free tickets to as many studio audience shows as possible and simply observe. (You might get lucky and find a bored floor manager who will show you round, but don't bank on it.)

A good way to get involved, see what's going on, and be paid, is to be a TV extra, or 'Supporting Artist'. In these post-closed-shop days, you do not need to be a member of Equity, you do not even need to have an agent, as some casting departments of TV stations will hire you direct. Years ago, I worked for a few months as an extra in Granada's *Coronation Street*. I was herded around with the other extras, and there was a lot of hanging around in changing rooms, but the experience was invaluable to show me what people did in a TV studio, and to get the feel of a programme being made.

Contact the casting department of your local TV station and ask about extra, walk-on (where there's an action you're directed to do) and small speaking parts. You may not have the opportunity to impress, since supporting artists are never directed to detract from the main action, but all experience is good experience, and you might be lucky and make that contact you need.

When on TV station premises, always carry a pen and paper in your pocket; not for autographs, but for writing down the names of production people you meet. Even if they can't help you directly at the time, it's worth keeping in touch with the odd phone call to find out what's happening with staff and programmes.

You will have a lot of setbacks; everyone does. However, if you really believe that you have something to offer, an opportunity will come your way eventually. There is an old saying, 'Talent always rises to the top.' Let me add another one here: 'Never hide your light under a bushel.' Just think: right now there could be a TV producer, sitting in an office, waiting for someone just like you to come along.

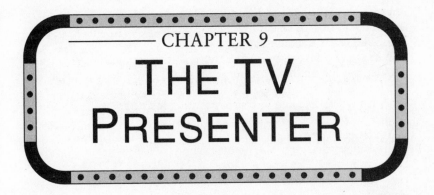

CHAPTER 9

THE TV PRESENTER

VIRTUALLY EVERY TV PROGRAMME needs presenters or on-screen reporters, and there are many people who feel that they could do the job, in return for the perceived high rewards and glamour. Of course, what seems a cushy number to the viewer at home can turn out to be nothing like that to the person in front of the camera juggling countless variables to give an impression of friendly composure.

The life of a television presenter must be one of the most varied on the planet. One day you could have the experience of a lifetime filming on a fully rigged nineteenth-century ketch on the high seas, the next you might find yourself hanging around bleak, windswept, concrete shopping centres in a godforsaken inner-city hell. I know such extremes can be true – they have happened to me.

Freelance presenters enjoy a great variety of work but may not enjoy the same job satisfaction as their colleagues on the staff. You might be hired for the day by a corporate video company. You would be asked to turn up at 8 am; you could well hang around until 11 or 12, then interview someone before lunch and in the afternoon do a couple of 'pieces to camera' that have been written out for you. Easy money, but not very satisfying if you can't contribute more.

You will find the best jobs are on those programmes where the presenter is involved at all stages in the production, where opinions are asked, ideas tested, rehearsals done. In this case you feel part of the team and gain increased job satisfaction. For this reason, it's best to try to get a contract with a TV station or independent company who are producing a series of shows for broadcast. You'll obviously get better exposure and security as well, if you go this route.

The absolutely worst jobs are those where the presenter is resented by others in the production team and overhears comments like 'All that money – and he's only worked five minutes today.' This can happen if a distant Executive Producer deems that a series should have a presenter like you, and happens to play golf with your agent. The people you are working with *really* wanted an animated talking sardine can – and if it *had* to be a human, you wouldn't have been their first choice. Nasty. All the joys of the special broadcasting version of office politics lie in the future for you, so don't say I didn't warn you.

Skills and qualities

Although there are many types of TV programme, all presenters need to possess certain general skills and qualities wherever they work. A good presenter should:

- Look right for the type of programme he or she is hired to present and have credibility, personality and presence.
- Have a clear voice that is pleasant to listen to.
- Understand the subject they are dealing with and the audience they are presenting to. 'Authority' isn't a type of voice or an act; it comes from knowing what you're talking about, and being able to explain it convincingly to others.
- Be able to ad-lib around a subject calmly and coherently under pressure.
- Be able to ask sensible questions of interviewees, listen carefully to the answers and make minimum reference to any list of questions.
- Be consistently 'on form', even when ill, or in the middle of a personal crisis. The show must go on.
- Be capable of sight-reading scripts while making sure they don't sound 'read'.
- Have an accurate mental clock so they can judge duration in their head.
- Be able quickly to summarise a story or script at very short notice to camera.
- Know how to finish an interview and sum up an item to camera.
- Perform with confidence without being put off by the director's 'talkback' in their ear, or by the prompting device breaking down.
- Have a good memory, to remember what they have to say while the camera is on them ('doing a piece to camera') and to remember movements and actions decided by the director.

Presenter's gear

Whether you are about to start taping your own network series or only to make your own first audition VHS, you will need a basic kit of presenter's gear. (If you are freelance, all these things are tax deductible so keep the receipts.)

THE MOULDED EARPIECE This will fit snugly into your ear so that you can hear talkback from the studio control room (the 'gallery'), or an outside broadcast vehicle ('scanner'). Your local hearing-aid centre will squirt gunge in your ear and make a mould. In about a week you will get a clear or flesh-coloured earpiece with a tiny flexible tube attached. This will connect to the talkback equipment.

Ask for earpieces for both left and right ears. You may lose an earpiece or get an infection in one ear. Also you may *need* two – I had a stint reading regional news bulletins where local gallery talkback was in the left ear while London network talkback was in the right . . . and I still had to concentrate on the script!

If talkback sounds faint, don't blame the engineers straight away. Wax builds up easily in these earpieces, so soak them in warm water and wash gently. If you are new to earpieces, and worry that you'll be put off by directors and production assistants talking in your ear, train yourself to listen and speak at the same time. Put headphones on, play a radio news bulletin in your ear and read an unseen script. You should be able to read, make sense *and* understand the news. It is possible, try it.

FACE POWDER Presenters of both sexes need powder of some sort under TV lights. You may have your own make-up people, but if you haven't, any kind of powder that matches your skin tone will do. Dab some on the shine zones: nose and forehead. Press in hard around the hairline where you will need good cover when you start to perspire. When shooting outdoors, shine isn't a great problem since the light is more diffused, but when the little portable 'handbasher' light comes out, reach for the powder puff.

BRUSH AND HAIRSPRAY Shine on hair is always emphasised and can look terribly greasy under television lights, so select a hairspray that gives a natural matt look. A vented brush and a *tiny* amount of spray should be all you need. Try spraying the brush, and then styling. Only spray directly on the hair when you're happy with the finished style.

POCKET MIRROR   Essential for studio work. Don't rely on others to tell you if your nose is getting shiny or if your tie is crooked. Use your pocket mirror in between takes or items. You might be able to see yourself on a studio monitor, but adjusting your clothing looking at yourself in a monitor is a bizarre experience. We are all used to wrong-way-round mirrors, but television monitors are right-way-round!

STOPWATCH   Every second counts in broadcasting, so unless you're happy with using a wristwatch, invest in your own stopwatch, which you may need to time movements and pieces to camera out on the road. I've found that some of the cheaper digital versions tend to fall apart after a few rough location shoots. You only get what you pay for.

AUDIO CASSETTE RECORDER   A small machine that takes standard-sized cassettes is an extremely useful tool for the presenter. As well as using it to record ideas or notes, while 'on the road', good television news reporters use one to record interviews, duplicating the TV camera's recording. Then the whole recorded interview can be played in the car going back to base to save 'thinking time' when you are editing.

PROMPTING DEVICES   Nobody has a perfect memory and television presenters usually get finished scripts on the day of recording or transmission. It looks bad if the presenter constantly looks down to refer to scripts. Eye contact with the viewer is very important, so in the studio, or in a controlled location, prompting devices are used. At the presenter's end, the device over the camera lens consists of a glass plate angled at 45°, to reflect a reversed horizontal screen under it. The words are scrolled up the screen and the presenter simply reads them, giving the impression that he or she is speaking without prompts.

The two main systems in use in the UK are made by Autocue and Portaprompt. In the old days, some poor soul had to retype the presenter's script onto a roll of white paper that was fed under a TV camera connected to the monitor displayed in the presenter's eyeline. Not only did scripts have to be typed twice, but when the job was rushed, words or even whole paragraphs could be left out, so the prompting roll had to be checked constantly. If the order of stories or script sections changed, the paper was literally cut and pasted back together in the new order. These joins often broke while the paper was being cranked through on-air, leaving the presenter with a blank prompting screen!

These days, scripts typed into a computer are printed out as hard copy as well as being electronically translated into moving words on the prompting screen. The advantages are obvious – less work, no mismatches. Everything typed on the script appears on the prompting screen. The size, brightness and contrast of characters on the screen can be changed, and script order changes can be effected by pressing a few buttons.

TIPS

- ☑ Don't worry about your eye movements as you read the words using a prompting device; unless the camera is very close, they'll not be noticeable.
- ☑ Read naturally; don't go faster because you fear the words will disappear. Trust the operator to follow your speed.
- ☑ Look relaxed and don't stare at the screen. If you are tense, force a few blinks or even glance away if it's relevant to the script.
- ☑ If the machine goes bananas and puts up the wrong script or, even worse, random computerised nonsense, go straight to the hard copy script and when looking up at the camera focus your eyes behind the prompt screen so the wrong words won't put you off. You should always have the right part of the hard copy script ready for emergencies like this, so make sure you turn pages, even if you're reading from the screen.

'HÖRTOCUE' On location, it may not be technically possible to lash up prompting screens, so if you find it difficult to remember long pieces to camera, connect your earpiece to a mini cassette recorder. Go somewhere quiet and record the required script section, preceding it by a 3-2-1 cue. Over-exaggerate the diction: it must be recorded clearly. Now put the script aside, rewind the tape and play it into your ear, repeating everything you hear.

This system, called 'Hörtocue' (after the German verb *hören*, to hear), scrambles your brain at first, but with practice you should soon get the hang of it and give a natural performance. The trick is to relax and let the part of the brain that is 'reading' the information from the earpiece get on with it while most of your attention is given to delivery. If you concentrate too hard, your eyes may glaze over or you'll simple stumble.

Before going in front of the camera, hide the tube and wire neatly away, and put the tape recorder into play/pause mode before stashing it into a back pocket. If you don't have a suitable back pocket, Velcro it onto the back of your jacket. When the director shouts 'Action!', simply flip the pause off, and off you go, repeating what you hear in your ear.

This system is very useful for moving shots, where you cannot maintain eye contact with the camera. You may be directed to walk through a door, look at paintings on the wall, walk down stairs, and then insert an eyepiece into a reflecting telescope . . . (like you do), while talking all the time. With your mouth automatically repeating the recorded script in your back pocket, you can concentrate on any movement you are required to make, without having to think too much about what words are coming next.

Presentation self-training

If you have never presented before, and are worried about how you'll come across at an audition or recording, it really can help to take a leaf out of the training manual of the Rupert Pupkin School of Television. If you've seen the film *The King of Comedy*, you'll know that Robert De Niro plays the part of a desperate prospective TV presenter, who has a mock chat show set in his bedroom. I'm not suggesting that you go to the extent of creating a cutout of Liza Minnelli to interview, but by borrowing or hiring a domestic video camcorder with a clip-on microphone extension, you can practise and review in privacy.

Read stories from the newspaper to camera. Talk to the lens about how you feel on issues. Pretend that you are a continuity announcer introducing various shows. Then play back the tape. Be tough on yourself.

Of course, the technical standards will be poor, but you will notice all the things you'll have to iron out in your presentation style. All this may seem rather childish and like 'playing television', but it is far better to discover faults at home than after you've blown a golden opportunity at a TV audition.

MOUTH AT FULL SPEED – BODY IN SLOW MOTION
Viewers see you in the confined space of the rectangular frame around you, so movement is exaggerated. Some presenters have an annoying and distracting habit of bobbing about in the frame on the close-ups. Imagine a steel rod up your spine. Make your head rigid, then relax a little to give what will appear to be natural movement on the screen. Watch a network news presenter tonight, and you'll see a mouth at full speed and a body in slow motion. You'll see a steady head, unhurried

arm movements and a relaxed professional look, all contributing to the required air of authority.

NEVER CROSS YOUR LEGS
If you are sitting at a studio desk, your centre of gravity won't be central with crossed legs and head turns will be harder to keep even and natural. Breathing will be more difficult too.

DEVELOP A RAPPORT WITH THE CAMERA
Look directly into the centre of the lens and imagine you're looking into a friend's eyes. Don't stare and don't let your eyes wander so you lose the viewer's attention. If a prompting screen is used, you won't see the lens, but don't worry: read naturally and ask the director to tell you if your 'eyeline' is off-centre.

HAVE EMPATHY WITH THE VIEWERS
Imagine the type of person who is watching your programme, and relate to them. On close-up shots, minor facial expressions can be real giveaways to your true feelings. Experienced presenters will put on a 'concerned' tone for a crash story, and a more lighthearted expression for the weather. You must become virtually emotionally involved with each story to come across sincerely and effectively.

MARK UP YOUR SCRIPTS
This involves seeing which sections are yours and marking a bold vertical line by the side. Then look at the sentences and divide them up. If the Autocue fails or you need to *précis* the script at short notice, you will be able quickly and easily to see the sentences in blocks. Next, study the words and check you know the pronunciation of every word. Double-check names and ask for a phonetic version to be put on the prompting screen if you think you're going to get it wrong on-air. Finally, divide up any complicated multi-syllable words into their components to make sure you say them clearly.

SPEAK TO THE RED LIGHT
Studio cameras have red lights on the top, which shows when they have been selected by the vision mixer. The red lights may be switched off due to reflection problems. If you don't have these lights, you only really know you're on if you see your face in a monitor.

Nothing looks more obviously wrong to a viewer than a presenter who is looking at the wrong camera. Directors and vision mixers can sometimes get their wires crossed and the director tells you to read to camera 3, while the vision mixer, following a rehearsal script, selects camera 2. You might choose to ignore the director because you see the red light on top of camera 2, but then the vision mixer switches up 3, having been kicked in the shin by the director. The director then realises camera 2 *was* the correct shot, because camera 3 has to be released to 'crab over' to the other side of the studio for the next item. You, the presenter, are left on screen playing camera tennis, not knowing where to look.

If you do experience a situation like this, or you get confused yourself, simply read from the script in your hand for the few seconds it will take for order to be restored in everyone's minds.

TURN ON CUE   On a live studio programme, if you stare into the camera waiting for your cue from the director, be aware that the vision mixer may cut to you early, and you will look a lemon. It looks much better if you turn your head towards the camera on cue; it looks as if you've been looking at another presenter or watching the previous item on a monitor.

However, for recorded pieces to camera, always stare for a few seconds before and after your performance. This helps the video or film editor, especially if your face is being mixed into the next picture.

BE PREPARED   When reading an introduction to a pre-recorded insert or report (usually referred to as a VT, videotape), always write another few words in case the tape is run late. Normally a videotape will be 'parked' on pause, five seconds before the first picture, to allow any video wobblies to sort themselves out when put into 'play'. Betacart players are virtually instant-start, so if they go bananas when the button is pushed, we poor presenters don't even have five seconds to prepare an explanation or apology.

Have emergency lines in the back of your mind. Stand-up comics always have witty retorts to hecklers on standby in their brains, and good TV presenters should have a carefully worded filler ready in case an item goes down. It's a favourite trick at auditions to switch the Autocue off suddenly or not play the scripted tape. Professionals should calmly give an apology for the missing item, then go on to the next or 'standby item' script.

TRUST THE SOUND PEOPLE   If you are used to speaking close-up to microphones in radio work, it is a shock working in television where the tiny clip-on jobs seem hardly capable of capturing the full resonance of your wonderful voice. Trust the equipment and trust the location sound person to follow you with the long sound pole. The microphone on the end of the pole is highly directional, and any shaggy-haired covering is simply for wind protection.

Radio microphones are sensitive, so if you're given a radio microphone don't be tempted to shout, even though the camera crew may be far away. Speak normally, as everything should be picked up (including comments muttered under your breath about the crew!).

FIGHT FATIGUE   The facial lines of late-night partying might be covered up by make-up, but there's no substitute for a decent night's sleep, and a session of mouth-stretching exercises before going on-air. (See chapter 13 on *Using Your Voice*.) Long hours of hanging around in a stuffy studio or on location can take the edge off a fresh performance. When your turn eventually comes, wake yourself up by splashing cold water on your eyes and behind your ears and gargling to freshen the throat. On camera, slightly widen your eyes as if you're aroused by the lens. If you look slightly tired or hot and bothered, it will come across even worse on television.

TENSION SHOWS   Make sure it doesn't, by stretching like a cat and yawning before the camera comes to you. If you're nervous, don't for a split second think of the thousands or millions of viewers watching you. Remind yourself that it's just a job, and you get paid for doing it well.

CORPSING KILLS   It certainly will kill your career if you have a fit of the giggles halfway through a serious introduction. If you feel a laugh coming on, distract your brain by the pain of pressing one heel hard onto the other foot. Just the thought of losing your job and the shame is normally enough to bring you round.

PRESENTERS' DRESS SENSE   Whatever type of programme you front, it is important to remember that the way you look must never detract from your authority or performance. When selecting clothes, jewellery, make-up and hairstyles, therefore, you must ask yourself 'Is it appropriate?'

Many new presenters worry too much about their clothes, thinking that they have to be at the forefront of fashion every time they appear on television. In truth, most viewers will hardly notice if you wear very similar clothes for each programme. This is of course especially true for male presenters where one suit may look similar to another; women can usually get a higher clothing allowance to compensate for the fact that they won't be wearing the standard male suit. If your contract includes an allowance, you will find that spending it on three or four sensible outfits will be better value than splashing out on one designer creation.

Above all, the clothes you choose must feel comfortable, fit well, and, for most shows, look uncontroversial. Clothes choice is more critical in a studio situation where pin-sharp electronic pictures and well-lit sets show up even the slightest defect. If you are working mostly outdoors on location, you will probably be on screen for less time, and there will be enough distractions with weather and background movement to take away attention from your attire. Indeed, many male news reporters have a couple of suits and a raincoat, and er . . . that's it. What they say and where they say it to camera is important; that they've spent lunchtime in a top menswear emporium isn't. Practicality is paramount here. Winter filming out on the road necessitates a decent set of thermal underwear to cope with the inevitable hanging around.

When choosing an outdoor coat, it is best to select one of a soft material. A sound recordist will not thank you when your waterproof mountain coat rustles against your hidden radio microphone. Fluorescent or very bright colours are best avoided in outdoor wear, since you will usually wear these clothes when the surroundings are grey and dull, so your coat will steal the shot.

If you have been booked to present a series of programmes, work out which clothes you will need over the recording or transmission period. Being organised like this really pays dividends so that you don't have any last-minute worries about whether you wore that red tie on last week's show or not. Bear in mind that recorded programmes may need you in exactly the same clothes two or even three days running to match continuity. Buying a couple of identical shirts or blouses would save you a laundry problem.

Under bright lights, pure white clothes can 'burn out' or even flare. If the camera sets its exposure for your bright clothes, your face will be too dark. Wear light grey or even pastel shades, which can *appear* white on TV, and you will help the vision engineers make you look your best.

Fine stripes or mesh or check patterns can cause unsightly, throbbing patterns on the screen. Big, bold patterns come across well but tiny detailed designs can look like stains. Solid colours normally look fine on television. Beware of very dark colours as they look black on some receivers.

Earrings and other jewellery may cause sound as well as reflection problems if, say, a necklace is near a lapel microphone. Take alternative jewellery with you to all sessions.

Check whether the Chromatic Separation Overlay system (Chromakey) will be used. If so, make sure you don't wear the colour that is being keyed (usually blue): you don't want the weather map on your tie, do you? (CSO is explained in Factfile 4).

I don't want to give the impression that the choice of clothes for television presentation is all a matter of dull practicality. What you wear and how you look can complement and greatly enhance your authority and personality. To state the obvious, television is a visual medium and the way we see people on screen affects the way we feel about them. A producer in an audition may like your personality, what you said and how you said it, yet feel that something about your overall look didn't quite click.

Turn down the sound on your TV set and flick between channels. Now that you are not distracted by what they are saying, observe what presenters are wearing and how their hair has been styled. Do you agree with their dress sense? Is it, in your opinion, appropriate? Are you distracted by any jewellery or colourful elements? By closely observing others you will be able to get a sense of the visual language of television. It is a language that changes all the time, of course; for example, in the 1950s every man wore a suit on screen, even for sports or leisure programmes. Colourful pullovers were fashionable in the 1980s, and now solid colour jackets are back in vogue.

Once you have identified an image that you feel would be right for you and your programme, half the battle is won. Keep this image in your mind, because the second half of the battle begins in the clothes stores where you may be persuaded by friends or the shop assistant to purchase clothes that you are not quite happy with. Unless you have total confidence in wearing a new outfit, your overall identity may come across as rather an uneasy one.

Television presenters should remember the three Cs. When in front of the camera they should feel Confident, Comfortable, and Conformist.

- ☑ **Confident** – you feel at ease in your outfit and with your hairstyle.
- ☑ **Comfortable** – nothing should be too tight, hot or itchy.
- ☑ **Conformist** – if you dress or act the maverick, you may alienate yourself from the majority of the viewers.

The production gallery

The gallery is the long control room that is soundproofed from the studio itself, and may either overlook the floor or be to one side. Inside you will find a long console with a mind-boggling array of switches, faders and lights, a wall of television monitors, and people in chairs in front of all this lot screaming at each other, screaming down microphones to people in the studio or technical areas, or screaming at themselves. When it comes to communication between the gallery and yourself in the studio, you can usually choose whether you want to hear 'open' or 'switched' talkback. With open you hear everything going on in the gallery, and this may put you off. Switched talkback can only be heard when a button is pushed in the gallery. This way you will hear only instructions relevant to you. I personally hate to be cut off from the gallery, especially when things are going wrong, but sometimes the director insists so he or she can talk about me without me knowing!

Examples of earpiece communication to the presenter:

- ■ cues – *'Standby camera 2'; 'Coming to you, Peter'; 'And cue'*
- ■ countdowns – *'Run VT9; four, three, two, one . . . . up VT'*
- ■ general information – *'Peter; graphic ready, if you want to refer to it'*
- ■ interview instructions – *'Wind the guest up now - thirty seconds'*
- ■ warnings – *'The next item isn't cued up, introduce item 8 instead'.*

The following are the gallery personnel:

THE DIRECTOR   This person has to interpret the editorial brief for the programme in the most effective and creative way possible. The director calls the shots, and is in charge of everybody in the gallery and on the studio floor. It's a very difficult job, especially on a live programme, as he or she must keep calm and make the right decisions quickly.

THE PRODUCTION ASSISTANT (PA)   The PA is an essential part of the production team and in the gallery is the director's right-hand person. He, or more usually she, will have been involved in virtually all parts of the production, working closely alongside the director. Her job in the gallery is to time every section of the programme on one of her stopwatches, essential if pieces are being recorded out of sequence. Also she'll remind the director of what is coming up next in the running order and may even tell the camera operators when they're on-air, via the talkback, although some directors prefer to do this themselves. The PA will certainly count down out loud into VT or film inserts.

VISION MIXER   There has to be excellent communication between the director and vision mixer, who needs to be virtually an extension of the director's body. The job involves punching up camera or graphic outputs to the main output of the studio; you have to have lightning-fast reaction times.

Here are some of the commands the vision mixer will hear, and have to put into action: *'Cut'*, *'Wipe'*, *'Mix'*, *'Super'* (Superimpose), *'Fade up'*, *'Fade out'*, *'Fade to black'*, *'Insert'* (Captions), *'DVE out'* (Digital Video Effect the picture - like spin and turn away).

PROMPTING DEVICE OPERATOR   A very important person for the presenter in the studio to get to know. Usually female (I don't know why), she normally sits in a gloomy corner of the gallery with her machine, the Autocue, Portaprompt or whatever. The programme's script will have been typed into the device, or transferred from the programme office computer. Her job is constantly to update the script as it changes (and it *always* does), and thus change the information that the presenter sees on the prompting screens in the studio. The talkback system should allow conversations between presenter and prompting device operator, so any alterations to script or typeface can be discussed.

A cog in the machine

When you get your first TV break, your ego may be deflated when you realise that you are 'just' part of the programme team. Even when you become someone the public want to read about, the camera people, director or make-up people won't fawn over you and pamper you all day. You are the presenter – you do your job, just as everyone else on the team is doing his or her job. It's simply that your mistakes are more public!

It's a fact of life that even though a rubbish collector may be more useful, a doctor may be a life-saver and a priest may be more spiritually uplifting, television presenters get more than their fair share of remuneration and public interest for the simple reason that their faces are regularly seen in that haunted fish tank in the corner of the living room. If you are a relatively well-known TV presenter, the smallest bit of tittle tattle will become a news story for the press, your name will go on the mailing lists of book and record companies, you'll start to get letters from charities and public relations companies wanting your help – all because you present a television programme. You may love all the attention, but please don't abuse the privilege by calling up for endless freebies, or by letting down organisers of events. In the long run it really pays to be honest, punctual and human.

CHAPTER 10
THE VIDEO SHOWTAPE

NOW YOU'RE ALL primed up and ready for that first opening – but what if the opportunity appears as an advertisement along these lines:

An exciting opening awaits the presenter of this original new television programme . . . Send CV and VHS to . . .

In other words, it appears that they want someone with experience: someone who has already collected their presentational greatest hits on videotape. What if you haven't a VHS showtape but you know you would be suited for the programme? You may even be a highly experienced radio broadcaster or live performer, but if you haven't already been on television, you are simply left with a jiffy bag with nothing to put in it.

This chapter assumes you haven't yet collected any past glories on tape. What should you put on your showtape? Let's start with a few things you should *not* include:

☒ HOME VIDEO CLIPS

No! The speech you made as best man at your brother's wedding may be hilarious to your family, but any home video is likely to be fuzzy, wobbly and totally unsuitable to show you off as a future professional presenter.

☒ PROGRAMME AUDITION TAPES

No! You may have pleaded with the television station to give you a copy of an audition you did for them, but:

(a) You were probably very nervous on audition day.
(b) Things they get you to do at auditions are never very inspired.
(c) Why show off the fact that you didn't get the job?

The purpose of the VHS showtape is to make you look at your best in a wide variety of situations, so unless you really are pleased with an audition, leave it on the shelf.

☒ WALK-ON AND EXTRA WORK CLIPS

No! Why show yourself in the shadow of a star? You may have felt chuffed to see yourself as an extra in a big production, but your showtape should show *you* upfront.

Aims of a video showtape

- To show that your face looks good on screen. By this I mean sincere and not shifty; pleasant and not repellent – a face full of personality and not characterless.
- To show that you have the skills required: that you can ad-lib, read autocue, interview people professionally and display all the skills that we have discussed in the previous chapters.
- To show how creative and how imaginative you are. By sending a self-produced cassette, you will be showing both these skills.

Creating the tape – your options

- You could ask a production company to write, direct, produce and edit your showtape. The technical quality should be excellent, although you will pay for all the expertise you are hiring. You should budget at around £2,000 for this. This option, of course, won't demonstrate your imagination or creativity.
- A cheaper alternative is to write, direct and edit it yourself, but hire a professional crew for the production. You could write a script, visualise it and then get the professional crew to video it for you while you direct. You could then hire an editing booth to put together your final showtape. This would cost around £1,000. The disadvantage here is that you may be a great presenter, but a rotten writer or director. What skills are you trying to show?
- The cheapest option is to write, visualise and direct your own script and produce it using a VHS or Hi-8 semi-professional camcorder which you could hire for a few days. You could edit it by using the pause button on your home video recorder. The

expenditure is now down to around £50. Of course, the technical quality will be pretty awful, you won't be able to add captions or music successfully or insert video effects, and, if you are presenting, who is operating the hired camera? The guy you met in the pub with the shaky hand?

My cheapest option shouldn't be dismissed out of hand. You may know someone who is a skilled camera operator; you may have great original ideas and don't want anyone else misinterpreting them. And – more likely – you may not have £1,000 to spend. If you choose option 3, hire the best quality camera and use the best editing facilities you can afford. This is especially important when you play . . .

THE GENERATION GAME Video can't be physically cut like film or audio tape. The bits you want from original tape have to be copied onto another tape in the order you want. This new tape, being a copy, will be one 'generation' down from the original and, unless you're using digital video recorders, the picture will look grainy, saturated colours may flicker, and sound may become muffled. Making the VHS copies from your finished edited tape puts you yet another generation down, and these are the cassettes that you will send out to prospective employers. Do you really want them to see your best performances through a fuzzy haze of video distortion?

Recording and editing the original action on a professional tape standard such as High Band U-Matic, Beta, Beta SP, one-inch tape or, if you can afford it, one of the digital formats, will give pictures of broadcast-standard quality, so VHS copies from the edited master tape will be excellent.

Semi-professional mediums like Super VHS, Hi-8 and Low Band U-Matic will give grainy but acceptable copies.

Using domestic VHS cassettes all the way through the chain will give very poor technical results. However, if cost really is a problem, get the best quality you can on VHS by:

- making sure your camcorder and editing gear are in good working order
- cleaning the heads of all players and recorders in all the machines you use
- using the very best quality cassettes you can afford
- switching *off* all the audio limiters (not forgetting those pesky automatic level controls which pump up the noise when they sense a gap. After a few generations, the sound becomes strained and muffled. Ride levels manually!)

■ Switching *on* all the Dolby switches if they are there. This will increase the signal-to-noise ratio of the sound tracks, thereby reducing background noise from the equipment.

THE PROFESSIONAL TOUCH   Look in the *Yellow Pages* under 'Video Services' and you should find a selection of facility houses: these are independent companies who offer editing, graphics, recording and, sometimes, studio and cassette duplication services. Many of the top BBC and commercial TV programmes are put together at facility houses, perhaps because the in-house facilities have been booked up, or because the TV station hasn't one of the latest whizzo digital effects machines that seem to be so necessary these days. Facility houses are a great source of information and help through the minefield of technicalities; they should be pleased to give you advice. After all you may bring them a lot of new business when you've 'made it'!

Even if you are not using a broadcast-standard tape, a facility house can sell you a VHS of professional-looking captions for you to edit on to the beginning and end of your showtape cassette. You may even want to show off at the beginning and give your potential boss ten seconds or so of professional test pictures called colour bars, along with a test tone. All these bits and pieces can be edited in on your home VHS recorder.

Make the most of whoever you know can help you. Don't work in a vacuum. Plead 'struggling potential television star' and you may get discount on an editing booth, cassette copies, or whatever. Friends may suggest angles to take or even think up great gimmicks when you're writing your script.

Ideas for a video showtape

So what do I put into my showtape? There are thousands of different answers to this question – one for each reader. *You* know your best points, *you* know the kind of job you're after. First, remember these points:

☑ Keep it fairly short – 8 to 10 minutes maximum.
☑ Put something really special at the start of the tape; that rewind button is so easy to push, and harassed producers are easily bored.
☑ Make sure you appear in virtually every frame. If you include an interview, for example, rough cut your interviewee's answers to

show it has been telescoped – the producer wants to see *you*, and your questions. The only exception to this is if you're showing your journalistic ability to a news editor. With news, you're quite often encouraged *not* to appear too much; many new TV reporters write in irrelevant pieces to camera just to get their faces on screen.

NEWS Against a plain 'studio' background, read an introduction to a taped story, to camera. Cut to your own report on a subject you have researched and directed yourself. Any subject will do, as long as the tape shows your skill at condensing a complicated story into a minute or two using attractive pictures and well chosen interview quotes.

HUMOUR / GAME SHOW / PERSONALITY The sky's the limit with this sort of tape. You might like to interview yourself dressed as a character, or edit zany sketches together. Get ideas from existing television shows, but obviously don't blatantly plagiarise.

Producers of light entertainment programmes are looking for versatile professionals who genuinely like people. So don't worry that you can't create a game show set in your living room – why not display your personality by doing a *vox pop* with shoppers, dressed as a chicken or a stick of rock?

Play practical tricks with a hidden camera. Perform a piece to camera changing characters as you change hats. Pontificate on life from your back garden deckchair. You know the style that would be right for you. You know what sort of show would best suit your personality, and what you can get away with.

MUSIC SHOW If you love music, let it show. Get permission to film in a record store when it is quiet and talk to camera about the new releases. Interview artists – little-known local bands will be glad to help out! Keep it tight, keep it professional.

CHILDREN'S PROGRAMME Produce your tape in the style of the programmes you are aiming for. There is no point mailing a zany, mad-cap showtape to a producer of a sober middle-class educational programme. To add life to your tape, rope in co-presenters if you like but make sure you look as though you are in charge.

PUTTING TOGETHER EXISTING CLIPS If you have already worked as a presenter and have some off-air recordings, there are still some things to think about.

Decide on your item order before you book the editing suite. What is your tape trying to do? You may love the lobster sketch, but putting it first won't help you get the part to interview the MD in that lucrative corporate video. If this is your target, you obviously need to select a 'sensible' extract first. Put any funny stuff last if you are desperate to show your versatility. Or make different versions; I have four different video showtapes, one for news, another for straight corporate presentation, and two 'personality' tapes with varying degrees of humour.

Professional touches. If all the pieces are from one television station, don't be afraid to put the station logo at the beginning and at the end. You must have it on VHS somewhere, even if you taped it before a programme. Use it mute if an announcer talks over the jingle. Don't forget to enclose a CV neatly folded into the library case. Talking of which . . .

'Case study'

I'm amazed so many VHS showtapes arrive on producers' or editors' desks in their shop-bought cardboard sleeves. Even worse are tapes dubbed onto low-grade tape with the chainstore name crossed out and the presenter's name scrawled across. I have honestly seen this – it's astounding. Why go to all that trouble making a tape, then let yourself down at the final hurdle? You are a presenter – so *present!* Sell yourself, not the manufacturer of the tape. Throw away the shop pack and invest in smart packaging.

WHITE CARD SLEEVES Tape duplicators and suppliers like **Duplication Express**, 9 City Business Park, Easton Road, Bristol BS5 0SP (Tel. 0117 9555599) will sell these to you for around 20p each. Neatly stick a typed or printed label on the front and don't forget the spine which will probably be the face seen when your showtape is stacked on the producer's shelf.

MOULDED PLASTIC BOXES Although bulkier and more expensive to post, these boxes give more physical protection to your cassettes as well as giving you an A4 size clear plastic wraparound in which to insert your letterhead, printed insert and/or photograph. Choose white or black plastic – they cost around 50p each. One of the biggest suppliers of these cases is **Quality Plastic Supplies**, Unit C, 2 Endeavour Way, Durnsford Road Industrial Estate, London SW19 8UH (Tel. 0181 946 8388). This company supplies audio and computer disk plastic cases as well.

VHS cassette duplication

If you have recorded your tape on a professional system such as Beta SP, you'll have to go to a video facility house where they'll charge you around £7 per VHS copy to duplicate from your professional master. It gets cheaper the more you order at one time, as with most things in life.

However, if you have a VHS cassette as your finished 'master', buy a bulk case of short blank tapes (Professional E10s are around £2 each) and hire a well-lined-up VHS editing suite to copy off. It's deadly boring copying one to one, but think of the money you'll save.

If you really can't afford an editing suite, borrow a friend's video and copy the tapes at home. Make sure all the heads are clean and the wiring is correct. Don't trail any of the audio wires near mains cables, unless you think that 50Hz mains hum on your showtape adds a certain *'je ne sais quoi'*.

'Return to sender'

Sometimes your VHS is simply returned with a curt 'Thanks, but no thanks' letter. This is why it's best to break the ice by phone before sending anything. Are they at least reasonably interested in seeing your tape? Maybe there genuinely won't be any vacancies for months.

You may be *asked* if you want your tape returned. Unless you're really hard-up, say *no*. Tell them to keep it on file, or joke that they can use it as a door stop. You wouldn't believe the work I have got from tapes I thought were 'dead' on people's shelves. They suddenly need a presenter and of course your professionally presented cassette is sitting up there on their 'pending' shelf.

Finally, always note down *who* you have sent tapes to, in the same book that you log phone calls and letters sent. Note which version of the cassette they've been sent and what reaction you have received. You must have an organised diary so you know who you can chase up and when.

CHAPTER 11
THE TV AUDITION

AUDITIONS ARE HELD to test the suitability of candidates for a variety of presentation jobs. Some television programmes audition newcomers and the system is also used for the more important corporate video or live conference work, but the majority of auditions are held for casting commercials and this chapter focuses on this area. TV and cinema advertising can be a lucrative line to get into and it's worth investigating before you get signed up into a broadcasting contract which forbids your appearance in commercials. A look through the archives discovers quite a few of today's well-known faces making their debut appearance in commercials. Even David Bowie starred in a TV advertisement for ice lollies before his music career really took off.

So what are the first steps? If you have an Equity card (details of joining in the Factfile on *Organisations*) and a suitable agent on your side who is in touch with the audition world, you have a huge advantage. There are very few advertised open auditions.

Auditions for any project can be embarrassing, humiliating and downright unfair, and it's only reasonable to warn you about this now. You'll find them held at TV studios, a hall hired for the day, or one of the specialist casting studios in London. For advertising auditions, you may have to perform one of a host of wonderfully dramatic non-speaking parts such as sitting down, opening a newspaper and reacting to a 'sale' advert; walking down a street munching a bar of confectionery; or placing a plate of dog food on the floor, 'creatively'.

You may wonder why they need to audition for parts which you feel virtually *anybody* could do. Well, you may look fine in a photograph, but it's whether you are convincing *in person* that matters. Also, the hiring of any facility/studio/equipment/crew is a very expensive affair;

they want to know that you are professional and co-operative *before* the shooting day.

The cynic in me would also say that Mr Ad Agency and Ms Client want to justify their important jobs and the huge budget they are pouring into the project. Studying you intently whilst you eat a cold piece of toast in ten different ways at an audition is one way of achieving this.

Casting for presenters for a TV programme is a much more in-depth affair. You may be able to memorise and read any script that you've been given, but it's personality and star quality which will be sought here.

Getting selected for audition

Whether you like it or not, everybody *typecasts*. Don't hassle your agent to put you up for every audition possible, because you won't fit into the producers' or agencies' idea of every type of character.

Get a pad of paper and list all the types of programmes and commercials you feel you'd be suitable to present. Be hard with yourself. Are you too old to do an upfront youth programme? Not sufficiently interested in science to present a documentary on cosmology? Too rough a diamond to present a slick game show? This will give you and your agent a good idea of the types of programmes to target and the ones to avoid wasting time on.

Now, check your versatility for on-screen commercial parts. List all the *types* of people you could play. Forget about lines, it's *how you look* that counts at first. Are you:

- a sensible-young-mum type, or a streetwise-raver type?
- a jack-the-lad type or an executive-businessman type?
- the rugged-macho type or the wimp-next-door type?
- the smoky-pub type or the exclusive-wine-bar type?

Think of all the stupid stereotypes we all have in our minds of what these people *should* look like and ask yourself if you really would fit the bill. Again, discuss with your agent the types of auditions to zero in on.

The phone rings

Usually you or your agent will receive full details of what you will be expected to do or say. You may have a script which has to be memorised. Sometimes you get nothing – in which case you *must* find out:

- What is the programme about, or what is the commercial product? How do you pronounce it?
- Who is it aimed at? Is it a specialist programme for enthusiasts, a daytime show for casual viewers, a youth programme, etc? Is the commercial aimed at middle-class senior citizens, or upfront youths?
- What clothes do you wear? What type of person do they want you to be?

Deep down you may feel nervous. Make sure this *stays* deep down. As with most things in life, you'll perform better in a state of relaxed concentration, not in a state of blind panic.

On the morning of the audition, if you've been sent or faxed a script, continually perform it in front of a mirror, alone. At the end of each 'take', tell yourself in the mirror how well you've done, how perfect you are for the part, how you're going to floor them at the audition. After a good dozen times, you will have completely memorised your script, and associated a warm, confident feeling *with* your script. However, remember not to learn a script merely parrot-fashion. Ask yourself: *'Do I sound believable?'*

Then forget about the script until about half an hour before the audition. Self-doubt might creep in and your mind might swap words around. Have faith that the words are all there in your subconscious, waiting to come out on cue.

Never wear new clothes to an audition. A new shirt or blouse may feel scratchy and strange and you won't be 100% at ease. A new suit may have longer sleeves than you've been used to and you may unconsciously tense your shoulders up so that your hands can be free. Also, never eat a large meal or drink alcohol before an audition. No one performs at their best feeling 'blown out'. You may feel a drink will loosen you up but it will more likely slow you down and impair your memory. Even if you're auditioning for a beer commercial, do you really want the agency or producers to smell alcohol on your breath?

Check in a good quarter of an hour before you need to be there. You can relax from the hassles of travelling, have a coffee, and grab a longer pep talk from your agent if he or she is there, as well a finding out the latest gossip from the others. If you haven't been sent a script beforehand, it's obviously even more important to arrive early. If they give you a black look, complain that the train was early.

The waiting room

There is only one thing worse than going to an audition. It's going to an audition thinking that you haven't a hope in hell of getting that part. So, if you walk into the waiting room and see rows of well-known faces who are far more experienced than you, think on this: the producers could be looking for a genuine unknown, and you could have a better chance than the 'stars'. Of course, no experience is ever wasted, even awful, embarrassing and humiliating ones! Learn everything you can from this audition so you'll have a better chance next time.

You'll be asked your name and the name of your agent, and, if you haven't had it before, you'll be handed the script. You may also have a form to fill in, which will usually be for the casting agency's files. It will ask about recent commercials and projects you've worked on, as well as checking your special skills and clothing measurements. If time is tight, study your script, and forget about the form until *after* the audition itself. If there are any difficult pronunciations, *ask*. Even the receptionist may know if certain words have been fluffed all day.

If you were sent the script before the audition, you will naturally have learnt it. Don't waste time restudying the script alone in a corner. Talk to the others in the waiting room and do your best to put them off learning *their* script. More importantly, fish! Find out more about the programme or commercial you are auditioning for, the production team and any future projects that they know about. The other candidates might have information that you or your agent don't have. Obviously, don't give *them* any hot gossip or leads. In the world of broadcasting, everyone is for themselves.

If time is on your side before your name is called, escape to the washroom and wake your eyes up with cold water. If you're going to be under lights, put your face powder on to lessen shine, then give yourself a big smile in the mirror. You're going to knock them dead today!

Into the lion's den

The time has come, your name is called, and you enter the audition room. Remember, don't panic. Keep in your 'relaxed concentration' mode. Imagine you are one of your favourite actors / personalities if it helps to calm you down.

In the room, or on the set, you'll be introduced to a series of key people who could be the producer, executive producer, casting director, and, from the commercial world, the advertising agency account handler, casting agency person and maybe a representative from the client's company. Make eye contact with all these key people and look friendly and professional. Shake hands firmly yet warmly and try to remember names and faces.

Hand over your photograph, CV and VHS showtape if they haven't had it already. Once you're installed in the audition position in front of the video camera, they may take a video still or Polaroid picture for the records.

Next, you'll almost certainly be asked something like: 'Tell us a little about yourself' or 'What have you been working on lately?' Remember to reply *directly into the camera lens*, and not to the person who asked you the question: the recorder will almost certainly be rolling, without your being told. Your reply to this will be as important as your performance with the script. If they have had your showtapes and photos they will know your voice quality and looks; they want to know if *you* are right for *this* job. Tell them what they want to hear. I once lost an important corporate job because I didn't self myself well enough at this stage, even though I read the scripts competently. They didn't know until after they chose another presenter of similar professional reputation and age that I was better qualified to talk on their subject matter. So tell the clients about all the appropriate work you've ever done. Don't prattle on about irrelevant details, tell them why you'd be right for the project. *Sell, sell, sell.* Finish confidently and positively after about a minute. Always leave them wanting more.

Now comes the audition proper. Listen very carefully to what they want you to do and remember they want you to do as well as you can. Don't be intimidated, take your time and if you fluff a line or completely mess it up, stop, take a deep breath and start again, without asking permission.

Getting the words 100% correct isn't important at this stage – the script may only be a rough draft anyway. The people intently watching you are looking to see if you and your style fit in with their way of thinking. Relax and do your best.

If you're asked whether you'd like to see the video playback, say yes – you'll learn so much by watching yourself. Even if you know the audition is running behind schedule, try and milk as much time as possible. The longer you spend putting over a good impression, the better are the chances that your name and personality will stick in their minds, if not for this project, then perhaps the next one. Ask sensible questions with a 'genuinely interested' look on your face to stall the inevitable 'Thank you for coming.' Things like:

- *'How did you decide on the name of the product?'*
- *'What's going to be the competition on other channels?'*
- *'When does the series start?'*
- *'Great to see (sponsor) is involved!'*
- *'I bet the animation sequence will be difficult.'*

Sometimes, the video recorder is kept on after the main audition while the director asks you other questions. Turn to face the director when listening to the questions, but always reply *into the camera*.

Finally, when you've said your farewells and left the room, take a deep breath and find somewhere quiet to write down the names and titles of the people you have just met, together with any other information you've gleaned from them. Do this *before* it evaporates from your mind in a puff of sheer relief.

Ad-libbed auditions

You may get into the audition room to find that, amazingly, no one really has a clue what they want you to do. You may be asked to 'Do the introduction to a new quiz show aimed at teenagers' – no more information than that. Don't worry. This makes things far easier than having to work within the straitjacket of a script. Let your imagination go wild, and improvise. Make up the names of co-presenters, prizes, how the game works, and so on. It's the *style* they're looking for, not the content.

The recall

Sometimes the best three or four candidates are called back for a second audition. Don't get a new hairdo or wear different clothes, unless specifically asked. They liked you as you were the first time round, remember. Never get downhearted if you aren't chosen for a recall. You may have done a brilliant audition, but there may be good reasons why they didn't want you. Your agent might be able to find out the truth from someone on the panel. Maybe you wouldn't have fitted in with the co-presenter who had already been chosen, or the part could already have been filled, and the auditions were merely a way of keeping the unions and agents happy. Don't take rejections to heart and get right on with pushing for your next project.

If you get the job it's very important that you pave your way to future success. Unless it's a long-term contract for a TV series, remember that during the few days of shooting the commercial, corporate video, or whatever, all eyes will be on you. How you perform and behave will determine whether you'll be asked back again by the same team.

If you do well, they may call you up for their next project directly without having to call a formal audition. First impressions really count, so until they get to know (and hopefully like) you, you'll have to be on your best behaviour.

Conflict of interest

Never audition for a rival product to one you're already promoting. The original client may want you for another series of advertisements and there will be tears, much embarrassment and lawsuits all round. With programmes, check your contract or call up your producer if you want to audition for a show on a rival channel to the one you already present.

Golden rules for new presenters

- ☑ Learn your lines, even if a prompting device is available.
- ☑ Keep smiling, even if they change the script at the last minute.
- ☑ Learn to put up with hot lights and having to stand around in shot; it's what you're being paid to endure.
- ☑ *Listen* to direction. If you don't understand – ask.
- ☑ Be co-operative at all times. Save the prima donna behaviour for later in your career!.
- ☑ Exude a cheerful, confident air.
- ☑ Stay out of everyone's way until you're needed.
- ☑ Try to be as fresh for the twenty-eighth take as you were for the first!

CHAPTER 12

THE BREAK INTO NEWS

A GROUNDING IN JOURNALISM can open many doors in broadcasting. Obviously news programmes require journalists, but journalistic skills are also needed in all factual productions, in areas such as documentaries, and in consumer, political and educational programmes.

As a journalist, you must have an open and enquiring mind, an insatiable appetite for accurate facts, and a good memory. You should have an interest in all areas of current affairs and an understanding of the views of others. You should be able to represent these views in an unbiased manner, regardless of whether you share them or not. You should be persistent but not rude, sceptical but not cynical in your quest for facts. The real skill is in selecting and rejecting information from which to weave together a script or report to match your original brief. All the qualities described above are equally important when working on a small local newspaper or reporting for a network television current affairs programme.

TV and radio stations rarely hire people just to read the news. You normally have to research and write stories as well, unless you are a top anchorperson. If you're an actor, I'm sure you feel you could 'act' the part of a journalist on-air, but in truth a news background is essential in order fully to comprehend the implications of the story you are telling the listeners or viewers about, and to ask the right questions of live guests.

Teresa Driscoll is the co-presenter of the BBC regional news programme, *Spotlight*, which covers the South West and the Channel Islands. After successfully completing a training course approved by the National Council for the Training of Journalists, she worked for both regional and national newspapers before working her way up in London's Thames TV newsroom to become an on-screen reporter. Four years ago, she accepted the offer to front the BBC News programme based in Plymouth.

'It really grates when someone says to me, "Weren't you once a journalist?" My present job fronting *Spotlight* every night leads some people to think that I merely read other people's scripts off the prompting screen. Nothing could be further from the truth. Indeed I strongly believe that a solid journalistic background is essential on a live news programme. Actors could deliver scripted lines, but without a news background they'd be extremely vulnerable, especially during live interviews or when called on to handle breaking news. Understanding is all. The whole credibility of the programme would be at risk if a true journalist wasn't at the helm.'

Teresa has this advice for a potential news anchor who feels that image, voice and screen presence are more important factors than the words they are speaking: 'Poor delivery and a scruffy outfit can detract from a good script, but no suit or hairdo is good enough to make up for a bad script.'

Network news presenters are seasoned professionals with plenty of on-air and journalistic experience under their belts. A huge responsibility rests on their shoulders to get it right first time, and be able to work under extreme pressure when stories are changed. Network news presenters regularly have to conduct live interviews with correspondents or politicians and a thorough understanding of current affairs is needed. Newcomers would never be offered an opportunity on a network news programme straight away.

Not everyone can make the grade. Finding out and writing about stories isn't always exciting or even interesting, and, as in most areas of broadcasting, taking on journalistic work means a willingness to accept irregular hours and an ability to work under pressure and to deadlines.

How they made the grade

ITN's Nicholas Owen worked as a newspaper journalist for fifteen years until he made the decision to cross over into broadcasting: 'Having decided to move into television journalism, I went to the BBC, walked through the front door and said, "What can you offer me?", which was probably terribly forward of me, but anyway . . . They asked me if I was prepared to work anywhere and of course I said yes. They sent me up to Newcastle for an interview and I was offered a six-month contract as a regional journalist – very much a back-room job. I went there not being sure of the route I would take, although I'd always thought I'd like to be a presenter. Within a short space of time I was doing on-screen reporting and I was then asked to do some presenting.'

How did he cope with the move from the written word to live situations in front of mass audiences? 'I had done a lot of amateur drama. Newscasters aren't actors, but there is an element of performance, and a certain sense in which you're entertaining people, holding their interests.'

So what advice would Nicholas give to people now? 'There is no substitute for a thorough grounding in journalism. These days that doesn't have to be print journalism – you can gain experience in local radio and TV stations. It is extremely unlikely that a pretty or handsome face will just walk straight in as a presenter. You can't beat journalistic training and on-screen reporting experience as preparation.'

The BBC's Martyn Lewis gives this advice for potential newscasters: 'If I knew the formula of what made a face work on TV, I'd bottle it. But the point is no one knows. What is really important is that ability to communicate with the audience. I know that lots of people go straight into the BBC as trainees now, but I think that nothing beats working up from the ground floor of your local radio or TV station.

'It is always possible to cross departments and spheres of work in TV. You can get in as one thing and move into presenting or newscasting from there. The BBC has now united the previously separate areas of news and current affairs, and the advent of bi-media, with radio and TV being produced in the same centres, also eases the passage from one type of work to another. The people who will succeed today are those who can adapt to the different disciplines of media.'

Nick Ross began his career in Belfast after graduating. As a BBC radio reporter, a documentary he made on the Troubles brought him to the attention of editors in London and he was invited to join *The World Tonight* and *World at One* on Radio 4. Helping to set up Radio 1's *Newsbeat* and working on a series of documentaries led him to an opportunity to co-present *Man Alive* for BBC TV. Other TV offers soon followed.

John Stapleton left school at sixteen and worked his way up the rungs of local newspapers, nationals and then through television research work before a reporting opportunity presented itself. He realises that it is a lot tougher for journalists these days: 'Now it seems a university education is almost vital for entry into the BBC. You'd have to be very lucky to do it the way I did. ITV is still more relaxed about these things and is probably a better bet for people who are starting out. And local newspapers and local radio are both very good ways of getting into the business.'

It is possible to move from general programming and entertainment into news. Paul Lockett, the morning news and sports editor of both Piccadilly Radio's AM and FM stations in Manchester is an excellent example: 'I have always been interested in news, but I really messed up an interview and was offered a technical operator job in the programming department. I was asked to record a showtape before I came in, and this so impressed the boss by its technical quality he must have thought that operating control desks was my forte. I protested that a news career was what I was really angling for, so he suddenly, and I thought very unfairly, asked me what was on the front cover of the *Daily Express* that morning. I was, and still am, an avid news reader, but that particular morning, I hadn't had time to even scan the headlines. "Not much of a journalist, are you then?" was the gruff response to my blank look.'

It took Paul ten years to make up for that mistake and to prove that he was material for the newsroom, and he ended up as a producer/presenter on daytime entertainment programmes, before applying to be trained as a journalist. After a short training course, learning the essential skills of shorthand, the law, and use of words, he was in. So what is Paul's advice? 'We get a lot of CVs through the Piccadilly newsroom which are all the same: a list of academic qualifications, but with no evidence of any relevant experience or personality. If people really wanted to work here, they'd badger for work experience in a real newsroom somewhere, or send us mock scripts they had written. We are a radio station – why don't applicants think of sending interviews or news bulletins on a cassette?' Paul says he can always tell if visiting students have what it takes: 'I ask them if they know the difference between opportunity and risk. An opportunity should excite you and a risk will worry you. If you feel good about the challenge of working in a broadcast newsroom, you'll relish the opportunity. If you're scared, you may never make the grade.'

TV and radio newsrooms do tend to have a fairly high turnover of staff, but you really have to keep your ear to the ground and constantly impress the right people to gain promotion; you have to jockey for position so that when opportunity knocks, you can take full advantage of it. BBC *Spotlight*'s Teresa Driscoll knew this very well in her years in the Thames TV newsroom.

'My first TV job after years in newspaper journalism was as a news researcher, which meant I had to check facts, set up filming and run round for the on-screen reporters. It was a responsible, satisfying job, but I was constantly yearning to be able to have a story all to myself;

to be able to stamp my own personality on reports, and, as icing on the cake, appear in vision. I knew that to get on in my career, I had to offer more than I was paid to do; whenever there was an opportunity to go out with a camera crew, I'd always make myself available. If there were late hours to be worked, I'd work them. This all paid off one day – I was working in the newsroom when a major newsflash had to be broadcast, and none of the on-screen reporters were around. Feigning complete confidence, I said to my boss, "Me! me! me!" and promptly found myself in front of a camera on-air. I remember my nerves being soothed by the director telling me in my earpiece "Super," throughout the bulletin; I only found out later that "super" didn't refer to my performance, but was a command to the gallery staff to put up a caption: "*super*imposition"! However, although that bulletin was a baptism of fire, it paved the way to regular in-vision reporting work, and eventually to my co-presenting the BBC news programmes for the South West.'

If your eventual goal is to be an on-screen network news reporter or presenter, it is very important to make the correct moves early on in your career. If you accept a junior job in a radio or TV newsroom, you will find it very difficult to become an on-screen reporter without a solid journalistic grounding. Virtually all TV reporters cut their teeth on newspaper, magazine, or radio journalism. If you are a school leaver with at least five GCSE passes (grades A—C, and including English), you can apply to newspapers to become a trainee. However, the demand for jobs is so great that most of the recruits are university graduates or have achieved at least two A-levels or equivalent. The same standards are required by organisations such as the **National Council for the Training of Journalists** for their one year pre-entry courses. The Factfile on *Training Courses* has further information on the NCTJ and other organisations which run journalistic training courses aimed at future broadcasters. The range of things you will learn as a trainee journalist will be vast, including aspects of law, public affairs and politics. You may discover that you have a natural affinity for a particular subject, which is often an advantage. Broadcasting correspondents have a broad journalistic background, but usually specialise in subjects such as education, social affairs, business, transport or the environment.

Routes for entering magazine journalism are the same as for newspapers; indeed, if you have any specialist interests you may find it easier to gain employment in publications which reflect these interests. Be aware, however, that a background in news journalism is more likely to impress broadcasting news editors than reporter work for, say, a caravan or electronics magazine. Women's magazines, however, are excellent training grounds for future TV feature and entertainment staff, for whom a flair for showbusiness and 'lifestyle' is a distinct plus.

Some big magazine companies provide their own in-house training, or send trainees on courses run by the **Periodicals Training Council.** (0171 836 8798). You might like to call the council direct for a copy of their *Training Course Guide* and *Magazine Training Directory.*

There are news agencies across the country which may take on trainees. Agencies like these do not publish or broadcast reports, but sell stories and pictures to organisations which do. Look up your local news agencies in the *Yellow Pages* in the 'News and Photo Agency' section.

There are also journalistic opportunities in public relations. Most organisations have PR departments and these people need to have similar journalistic skills to those already described. There may be a house journal, press releases or internal leaflets to write. The **Institute of Public Relations** can send you details of work in their industry. It may also be worthwhile contacting organisations which provide news services for other broadcasters; for example, **ITN** who provide news for ITV and Channel 4, **IRN** and **Network News** who provide this type of service for many commercial radio stations too small to have their own newsroom or who take this as a supplementary service. The *Contacts* Factfile gives a list of broadcast news services.

Getting the break

A post in either a BBC or ITV regional newsroom can be enormously rewarding and can be great discipline for tackling all sorts of other programmes. Responsibilities vary from station to station, but, as a news presenter/reporter, you would present bulletins which the rest of the newsroom have created for you. If you were sent out on reports, news researchers or regional journalists would do most of the setting-up work for you. You could be asked to voice or present other regional programmes, such as sport or documentaries, or to do some continuity work.

To target work in the regional TV newsroom, it is essential to know the programmes well before you apply. If you don't live in a particular area, ask friends who do to send you videos of bulletins and regional magazine programmes. You've got to get a feel of the TV station you're applying to. It's important to be familiar with the output if you are offered an interview with the editor of news; it would be very insulting if you weren't. You'd probably be asked your views on improving the programmes: what elements are missing, which features work the best.

A day in the life of a regional TV reporter

Let's assume that you have just attended the morning meeting where you have been given a brief by the editor or producer. The word 'brief' also describes the few notes you've scribbled down about the story and the angle your report has to take. Over the next seven or eight hours, you've somehow got to get a fully researched, set-up, written, filmed and edited item on-air. The first time you have such an assignment given to you, believe me, you will feel you have been given an impossible, insurmountable task. Every job, of course, becomes easier in time; just watch the seasoned hacks have a coffee and a general chat with their feet up on the desks before they even bother to make the first call.

Unless something has to be filmed immediately, you will usually have time to read any background information, such as newspapers or press releases. Then the phone-bashing begins in order to set up interviewees, source pictures, book lines, get props and to ask for a TV crew.

An average regional magazine programme has three or four crews on hand, consisting of camera operator and sound recordist, and you would book them at whatever location and time you needed them. Whether they actually turn up at this appointed hour or not is the first of many variables of your stressful day.

If the story is planned to be on-air that evening in the 6.30 pm programme, you would have to calculate all the time elements. For example, if an interviewee is only available after 4 pm, at a location twenty miles from the television station, you would first add fifteen minutes to allow for your guest being late and another fifteen minutes to talk to the interviewee before the camera rolls, while the crew set up the camera and possibly lights.

Add another fifteen minutes for the actual interview, the goodbyes and grabbing a few 'cutaway' shots which will help to illustrate your story (all the other shots, including pieces to camera, you would have tried to get beforehand) then at the moment the crew give you the master cassette and get off to their next job, you will have one and three quarter hours before your programme goes live on-air and you haven't even reached base yet.

Don't worry. You would have already contacted your base to tell them what time you'll be back at the television station and asked them to book you a place in the sound studio to record your commentary, and an editor to cut your story together. You may also want the film and video library to dig out shots you may need, and the music library to find any music.

On the journey back to base you would listen to an audio cassette of the entire interview which you would have recorded at the same time as the one on the master video cassette now sitting on the passenger seat. Obviously you can't write notes or use your stopwatch whilst driving, but you can play the audio cassette again and again until you know the interview inside out, so when you set foot into the editing booth, you'll know exactly which bits to use and which to reject. You are looking for key sentences, or 'soundbytes'.

As you get more experienced, you will learn to recognise how long each soundbyte is, and you will be able to guess accurately the final length of the whole report. In the morning meeting you would have been given a duration along with the story: say, three and a half minutes for an in-depth feature, ninety seconds for a reaction piece to a topical story.

After screeching to a halt at reception at 5.15 pm, and racing in with your precious tape (and encountering the surly security person who wants to see your ID card even though he sees you every single day), you would head towards the sound studio to record your commentary.

5.30 pm, and there's no time even to grab a coffee. Racing down the corridors, you take your commentary audio tape, master videotape, library shots and music (if needed) into the video editing booth where an editor should be eagerly awaiting you.

Oh, and don't forget to take your thinking head into the editing booth, along with all your notes and tapes. Your editor may not have a clue what you have actually shot, so it is up to you to direct him or her to cut together the story with the help of the news producer, who will no doubt be popping in to all the editing booths to check on how the various stories are progressing.

Editing videotape at such a late hour, you cannot afford to make mistakes. The pressure can be very exciting: will this story make it to air? If you have been assigned two minutes and you edit together two and a half minutes, the programme will have a serious timing problem and you will be in serious trouble.

Your story is too late to be included in the full rehearsal which began at 5.45 pm. The presenters who have been sitting all afternoon in a hot studio will have a moan at you.

You race to the videotape play-in area with the clearly labelled cassette of your finished, edited report. Complicated graphics and captions may have to be mixed in live on transmission through the gallery, or control room.

6.10 pm. Back in the newsroom, you log into your computer, and write a caption list for your story. You also agree on the introduction script which the news producer will have already written. The introduction script will be given to the studio presenters as well as all the staff in the gallery. The presenter's words will also be included on the prompting computer.

6.20 pm. Although your script has been automatically accessed by the prompting computer's operator for the presenter to read off the screen, nobody has a paper copy of the script and the director in the gallery is screaming for it on talkback.

6.25 pm. The hard-working newsroom photocopier grinds out the copies of your script, and because the newsroom runners have disappeared, you have to distribute them yourself.

6.30 pm. You slump in a newsroom chair and watch the programme on the off-air monitor, and hope your story makes it on-air.

And tomorrow . . . it's all going to happen again . . . with a completely different story and a different set of variables.

Could *you* cope with the stress of a job like this or the frustrations of missing that evening deadline? You may work your guts out all day to find your story has been pulled at the last moment to make way for a more important one. A balancing interviewee doesn't show up, leaving it too late to set up another one in time, effectively scrapping your item.

A reporter's life can be very taxing but some people thrive on the uncertainty and challenge of producing a quality, topical story under such tight deadlines. Of course, you won't have a last-minute story to cover every day, and you may occasionally even have time for a lunch break. But don't count on it.

Advice for newsreaders

KEEP TO THE ORDER OF THE PAPER SCRIPTS

You may have ten stories and thus ten scripts in front of you. If you're on TV, all these will usually appear on the prompting device in front of the camera.

At the end of each story, look down and slide the script you have just read to one side, revealing the next. Never *turn* paper during a bulletin; always *slide* to minimise paper crackle.

Make sure the correct script is always in front of you, even though you don't normally read from it – you will be looking up and reading from the autocue. The reason for this is that if the prompting device fails whilst you are live on-air, you can immediately glance down and pick up where you left off.

LOOK UP WHILE SCRIPT-READING   If a prompting device is not available, or has gone wrong, the best idea is to look down at the start of the sentence, and memorise as much as you can from that one glance. You should be able to remember at least six words – then look up at the camera to speak. On the fifth word, look down and pick up where you left off, glancing ahead to memorise six more words.

This may sound impossible to do, but it is fairly easy in practice. The art is to have the confidence to remember the words. Try it now; sit down at a table and pretend the camera is at eye level on the wall in front of you, and away you go with the next paragraph of this book.

Get into a rhythm of looking down and up. It's a bit like swimming, where you bob up for air, but in television newsreading, your 'air' is a glimpse at the words on your script.

A useful tip to make things easier is to separate sentences on your paper scripts with a drawn line. Then you can clearly see that you have, say, five sentences on one script. If you've looked up to read the end of sentence two, you know you have to glance down to the third block on your script, sentence three.

SORT OUT DIFFICULT WORDS   The newsroom should have supplied you with your scripts in good time so you can check pronunciations. If you don't like the way they are spelt, change them – the viewers or listeners won't know. For example, there might be a company called Strachan & Henshaw and the company pronounces the name Strachan in the English way: 'strawn'. Tell the prompting machine operator and change your paper script to the phonetic spelling, 'strawn', so you won't have a brainstorm and blurt out 'Strack-han'.

Make multisyllabic words easy; if, for example, you think you are going to fluff 'extraordinary', divide the word up like this: ex / tra / or / din / ary.

READ STORIES WITH CARE AND AUTHORITY   Bad newsreaders fall into the annoying habit of trying to sound like what they think newsreaders *should* sound like. They put on an overtly 'concerned' tone and read every sentence with the same speed and intonation, so the sense of the stories is hard to comprehend. The cure is to *understand* the stories fully, so your voice will naturally put emphasis on the correct words or parts of sentences. Get a feel for the story and think about the real people that are being affected by it, and it will show in the timbre of your voice.

MANAGE LIVE INSERTS

If you're about to hand over to a live reporter, liaise beforehand with them. Find out:

■ *where* they are and *who* they're going to speak to
■ *how long* they're going to talk for
■ what their final words will be. This is called the 'out cue'. It may by obvious, like: 'Back to you in the studio,' or 'More from outside the court later in the morning.' Sort out in your own mind what you'll do if the live link goes down.

Some radio and TV stations have an agreed 'SOC'. This stands for Standard Out Cue and usually means the traditional name / channel / place: *'Chris Vacher, BBC News West, Yeovil.'*

KNOW YOUR PROGRAMME

Insist on viewing/listening to at least the starts and ends of all the taped inserts before the transmission. You'll get a flavour of the reports so you'll know the style in which you should tackle the introductions and 'back announcements' (the reference you may make to the item just broadcast).

SAD OR HAPPY?

Remind yourself which are the light-hearted stories by putting a smiley face on the top of a humorous or warm-hearted script. I once launched into a 'kids doing good work for charity' script by using a tone of voice that made it sound like the children had been involved in an horrific accident. Bad news for me...

THINGS CAN GO WRONG

A taped insert may suddenly not be available, in which case you will be left in vision. I've seen some people assume that the insert is being shown, because it's on the script, and smooth their hair (or worse), thinking they were out of vision. The trick in TV is always to keep an eye on the 'off-air' monitor. You may have to suffer the confusion of many different screens around you showing different scenes – but if you see yourself on the off-air monitor, you're on the air, no doubt about it! I remember once waiting to hear my cue to speak to camera at a very noisy outside broadcast. The earpiece just wasn't loud enough to hear the director, so one of the crew held up a mini portable TV set. I spoke as soon as I saw my flickering face on the screen, and it worked fine.

In the radio world a red light in your studio should indicate that your microphone may be 'live'. Again, if you can ask to hear an off-air receiver in your headphones, it is a double check.

A live or taped piece you have just introduced may not appear for one of many reasons, technical or human. The way not to lose authority after reading an introduction to a non-existent report is to say something like, 'A *full* report, coming up soon.' You would then proceed to the next item. Remember that you'll need the script again to paraphrase from, when you are told that the report is able to be played. Place it to one side.

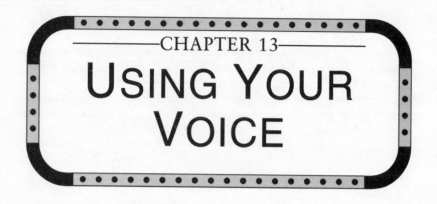

CHAPTER 13

USING YOUR VOICE

*N*O BOOK CAN SUCCESSFULLY train your voice, let alone one chapter, but I hope to give you a few pointers in the right direction. Like it or not, something about your voice may get on people's nerves. A well-rounded, resonant, friendly, clear voice is more in demand than thin, harsh, or garbled voice.

If you're a radio presenter, you'll know that by turning up the bass control on the microphone channel, and by switching in a compressor circuit, you can make your voice sound 'butch' and 'punchy'. Unfortunately, this can also make you sound muffled and flat if you're not careful. It is far better to train the voice equipment in your own body to create the desired effect.

Resonance

A resonant voice in broadcasting is extremely attractive in both men and women, and portrays authority and well-being. However, nothing is worse than a 'put on' resonant voice which can make presenters sound incredibly insincere. Here's how to develop your *natural* resonance.

VOICE EXERCISE: RESONANCE   In the morning, when your voice muscles are more relaxed, find a quiet room and sit comfortably. Softly hum the first note that comes into your head. Shape the sound like 'OM', tailing out the 'M' until you run out of breath. Don't worry if you're not musical; hum the 'OM' sound as best you can, and try to feel which parts of you are vibrating.

Now take the 'OM' progressively lower. If you are a musician, take the notes down in semitones. Go down the scale until you reach the lowest note you can chant without straining. Don't force it; the note should still be steady and recognisable. If you have a musical instrument handy, jot down which note you've reached.

The idea is that the 'OM' chant should resonate in your *chest* area rather than in your throat. The latter will produce strained vocal cords and simply not sound as good. The volume at this stage is not important, the key thing to aim for is *chest resonance* at your lower note, and to sustain it for the whole breath. You may find it easier to stand rather than sit down for this exercise. Breathe slowly and deeply from the stomach.

I know this is deadly boring, but try to do it for ten minutes a day; you should notice a real improvement in a few weeks. Concentrating on your breathing is good for the brain, will boost your energy, and is an effective and easy way to give your voice warmth, depth and authority without sounding phoney.

Soon your lowest note will go even lower, and your voice will have the ability to sound richer and more resonant.

How to switch it on before broadcasting? Simple. *Relax*. When you're stressed up, listen to the timbre of your voice: strained, high-pitched and thin. When you're with your lover at midnight in an intimate candlelit restaurant, how do you sound then? Exactly!

You may be wondering how you can relax in front of the microphone, cameras or audience. As time goes on, you will feel less and less nervous about performing; it will just become your job. When you're starting a new series or working on a new station, however, you're bound to feel tense; try all the usual calmers: whistling or humming a song, forcing yourself to sit in complete quiet for five minutes before the performance, thinking that it's only a job and you don't need the money, and so on. It's very important to relax to ensure that your full resonance potential is realised.

Clarity

There is little point in having a deep, resonant voice if it can't be understood. Many presenters on the radio make the error of gabbling, running words and sentences into each other, or putting on a lazy mid-Atlantic accent. Television presenters have a slightly easier time in vision, since subconscious lip-reading and watching facial expressions help the viewer understand what is being said. This is no excuse for sounding slurred, of course, and all broadcasters should constantly monitor themselves to ensure that they don't slip into bad habits.

Everybody has different reasons why they may not speak as clearly as they might: teeth formation, lack of confidence, laziness . . . and tiredness. There can be nothing worse than having to present a bright and zany children's TV programme or a fast-moving radio breakfast show when you've had a late night for whatever reason. Some people over-compensate and go wildly over the top to sound wide awake, and this can result in clarity of speech taking a back seat.

The following exercise will help you counteract a problem which, at some point, affects us all.

VOICE EXERCISE: CLARITY   Say aloud the letter: 'A'. Say it loud and say it clear. Really move the mouth and cheek muscles. Now say 'B'. Get those lips moving to produce a super-clear sound. Now smile like a Cheshire cat to say 'C'. Keep it loud and clear. Go through the entire alphabet in a similar manner, over-enunciating each sound as if teaching a child. If you do this first thing in the morning you'll be exercising muscles that will not yet have been used in the morning mumble around the breakfast table.

Repeat the entire alphabet, this time slightly faster, using all the mouth, cheek and tongue work you put in earlier. You should be able to speed up sufficiently to speak the entire twenty-six letters in ten seconds, without losing clarity. (I can still sound clear at 5½ seconds, but there again I haven't got a more creative party-piece.) This exercise is brilliant for unjamming a tired brain and mouth, as well as promoting general clarity and tight mouth control.

Sibilance

Sibilance can be a real bugbear of any broadcaster's voice. The 'splashy', high-frequency hiss surrounding any 's' sound can be really irritating and technically difficult to record. A badly tuned or cheap radio receiver can make a sibilant presenter sound even worse. A qualified speech therapist or even a dentist may be able to help a bad case of sibilance, but here's an exercise to help cut down that dreadful 's' sound.

VOICE EXERCISE: SIBILANCE   Say this:

*'Simply Super to See So many Scottish Sailors at STV's Summer
Special Spectacular!'*

Record it on a quality machine, better still in a studio, and analyse the result.

If you're not happy with the hissing 's' sounds, try again. This time try not to run all the words together, without making it sound too staccato or jerky. Also, speak as loudly as you can in the circumstances. Sibilance is much more pronounced at lower-volume speech levels. Cut down on the length of time you give to the 's' sounds in each word. Do this by mentally 'aiming' at the *second* syllable, not the first, if the word starts with 's'. Start off by saying 'Imply uper to ee o many ailors . . .', etc. Then reintroduce the 's' bit by bit, until the sense returns, but not the sibilance.

Spontaneity

Broadcasters and voice-over artists need to have mastered the skill of making their voice sound natural and spontaneous when they are in fact reading from a script. The skill is in reading as if the words are coming from the head, not the page.

We all know that newscasters are not ad-libbing – those bits of paper they shuffle during the end credits aren't their expense forms – but watch a top network news presenter tonight and you will hardly notice that he or she is reading from a prompting device. You will also feel the authority they are exuding. They speak as if they have a personal knowledge of each story of the day; in reality, many stories may be just as much news to them as they are to you. Late stories are often slotted into the running order at the last minute, and have to sound just as professional and authoritative as the ones which have been practised all afternoon. Chapter 12, on the News, gives presentation tips on this unique aspect of broadcasting, but all areas rely on scripts of one sort or another. The idea is to not to give the game away that you're merely reading someone else's words.

Listen to an inexperienced radio presenter change style from ad-libbing out of a fading record into a weather report, which has been faxed from the weather centre. You'll hear words the DJ would not normally use, like 'precipitation', 'occluded', etc, and the whole style will be stilted, slower, more obviously *read*.

Here's how to sound natural when reading any script, news cutting or other written material on-air.

PUT IT IN YOUR OWN WORDS   Change the script into something nearer *your* style, if necessary. Replace words and sentence constructions you wouldn't normally use. If you have any doubts that your changes may alter the sense of the piece, check with the boss.

TEACH YOURSELF TO READ AHEAD
This is essential on sight-read scripts. You should be able to look at and comprehend up to four or five words ahead of the ones you are actually speaking. You have to learn this ability to some extent so you can spot potential errors before you stumble. You'll also get the sense of the sentence correctly. If you put the emphasis on the wrong word, it's a real giveaway.

AD-LIB 'THINKING NOISES'
Try adding a few *minor* 'thinking sounds' like 'er', 'you see', 'mm', into a script. You'll sound as if it's coming from your head, not your piece of paper. (But, obviously, this *isn't* appropriate in a news bulletin or in voice-over work.) Don't get into the habit of using the same 'thinking noises' all the time.

VARY THE PACE
Go *faster* over obvious parts of sentence construction, *slower* over unusual words, phrases or facts. This is what we all do in everyday conversation, so adding this variation to a script helps to make it sound more natural.

SHOWCASING
Here's a technique used by commercial voice-overs – it's very useful for all of us. When a broadcaster has to pack a lot of words in, there's a danger that key words may be lost. In an average 'overwritten' radio commercial, for example, even the client's name may be slurred in the race to pack all the words into thirty seconds.

'Showcasing' is a technique in which certain words are highlighted without speaking them louder. Here's how to showcase: you leave a *tiny* gap before and after the selected word, and the word is also given a *slight* emphasis. The gaps are not long enough to take breath. Neither are they long enough to sound obvious to the listener. A professional commercial voice-over artist will automatically showcase certain things in a script, usually the product or the client's name.

I've only touched on the huge subject of voice skills and training. There are plenty of specialist books you can buy and classes you might like to attend. If you feel you do need more help in improving your voice, make sure the book you buy or the teacher you hire is relevant to your needs. A theatrical voice class may help you to recite Hamlet's monologues well, but may not help you pass the audition to voice the latest commercial for Nobby's grommets!

Voice-over work

Many radio and television presenters, and well-known actors, supplement their income by hiring their voice out for various projects. (There is also a small group of people who are full-time voice-overs, and do virtually nothing else.) This élite team stays élite because advertising agencies and production houses tend to use the same people most of the time. They know the work of their favourite voice-over and know how they'd handle the material, and many scripts, especially commercials, are often written with a particular voice in mind.

Another reason why there tend to be few successful voice-overs is that there are skills unique to this kind of work, and the simple truth is that not everyone can do it well. It's all very subjective, but if you really want to break into the world of the voice-over, don't be put off; the financial rewards can be phenomenal. Once you have voiced particularly successful videos or commercial campaigns, you could find yourself being asked back to do more and more.

Being offered some voice-over work can help in securing a presentation job. The people you will work with at the radio station's in-house production department will know all the latest gossip on who is leaving or whose ratings have been poor. Even at outside recording studios, you could make valuable contacts and your voice could be broadcast on just the station you'd love to work for. It's certainly a way to break the ice with the Programme Controller there.

So what qualities are required? Obviously, a clear, resonant voice is a real plus. Acting skills might be useful for character parts in commercials, but time is so limited in the world of advertising that all the timing, pace and character development which you learn in drama school goes out of the window. (Producer on talkback: *'Fit those last two lines into three and a half seconds, will you, lovey?'*)

Radio commercials in particular tend to be written using stereotypes such as 'George, the hen-pecked husband' or ''ello—'ello—'ello—policeman' and virtually anyone can ham-up these sorts of clichéd parts to the producer's satisfaction. This has come about because of the time restrictions. Subtle characters cannot be developed in a twenty-second advertising spot.

The voice-over's special skills

PATIENCE AND CONCENTRATION   Remember, you'll be stuck in a stuffy soundproofed booth with direction from the control room given over your headphones or speaker. Quite often clients are among the people who invite themselves into the control room, along with the producer and engineer, and all will be listening to your every nuance. A session with a room of backseat directors all chipping in with ideas is bad news. The worst is hearing a client in the control room exclaim that you're performing poorly, not realising that you can hear every word over your talkback headphones. You must keep your concentration even when repeating a short script for the umpteenth time with yet another slightly different intonation.

INSTANT ENTHUSIASM

Could you sound genuinely excited about *Brian's Plumbing Service*? If you can't, they will book someone who can.

VOICE VERSATILITY

To save money in radio commercials, they often ask you to play all the parts. Could you make your voice sound like two or even three completely different people? How are your accents? Could you read this paragraph in an acceptable Cockney, Bronx, Italian or Australian accent? Try it now.

Now read some sentences in character. Men, give me:

- an aged judge
- tramp in gutter
- smarmy game show host.

Women, give me:

- Bored shop assistant
- High-flying executive
- Offhand receptionist.

SPEED

In commercials, every split second counts. Scripts are usually overwritten and you may be offered a script which can be comfortably read in forty-five seconds but needs to fit into exactly thirty seconds. The skill here is in reading fast but not sounding rushed. Don't be tempted to shout or raise the pitch of your voice unless that is what you are asked to do. You'll end up with a sore throat and an ineffective advertisement.

You will find that you can read much faster if you *relax* the vocal cords, keep your pitch at the normal levels, and speed your *brain* up. If this sounds bizarre, it will all make sense after a lot of practice.

SENSE OF TIMING

Good voice-overs develop an accurate stopwatch in their head. They can sight-read a script and fit it into the correct time without even looking at the second hand on the wall clock.

Your sense of timing will have to be spot on if you are ever asked to fill in the gap in a pre-recorded sub-mix of a commercial. You may have exactly 4½ seconds to say your bit in between the sung sections of a jingle. Mess up any words and it's rewind time, along with black looks from the producer.

Now you can appreciate why the top professional voice-overs are used over and over again. Advertisers view newcomers as an unknown quantity – they may cost a fortune in studio hire charges, whereas the old pro.s can be trusted to deliver on the first take. But don't let this put you off – new voices have to come from somewhere.

John Mountford is the Managing Director of JMS in Norwich, an independent studio which produces a vast amount of radio commercials for stations all around the country. What advice does he give to people who want to do voice-over work?

'There is a significant difference between people who have a "nice voice", "read well", or whose friends tell them that they "ought to be in radio" – and a professional voice-over. Understanding how the tiniest alteration in inflection can make the difference between success and failure, why the producer or client needs a certain performance, and being able to pack it all into thirty seconds – *that's* a good voice-over.' Over John's twenty-one years in radio, he has seen the industry grow and grow; does this mean more opportunities for voice-overs? 'Certainly there are more commercials to be made, but there are also more people who want to make them cheaply, and are prepared to use an inferior voice-over artist. The "big" commercials still tend to call on real professionals and remunerate them accordingly.'

Vicki Robinson, Managing Director of one of the largest agencies for voice-overs, Voice Box, agrees. 'I would say that sessions at radio stations themselves have actually decreased; these advertisements are obviously still being made and I believe many stations are using their existing staff to voice things for free. This is a shame, because a good radio presenter does not necessarily make a good voice-over artist.' Vicki's agency has been established over ten years, and the voice-overs she represents come mainly from two sources: 'The skills required of a voice-over are similar to those taught to actors, so some of the artists I represent come from the theatrical world. Then there are the broadcasters, who have honed their timing, resonance and microphone technique to a standard required of the voice-over. An agent such as myself wouldn't really be interested in total newcomers until they had some experience under their belts.'

Voice work can be satisfying and lucrative, but most of the time it's not the gravy train some outsiders imagine. Tony Hawkins is a professional voice-over and has also been a TV continuity announcer and promotions voice-over on Channel 4 and Granada. 'Rates of pay have grown very slowly over the years and more and more untrained voices are being put on air. The general standard of commercial production at radio stations is abysmal – it wasn't much better ten years ago – and it's getting worse. Nobody really cares anymore.' Tony's advice to newcomers is straight to the point: 'If you go for voice-over work, be warned; the driving between the studios is exhausting and the clients will drive you bananas. Sometimes you are directed in voice sessions by vastly overpaid advertising agency executives who have as much idea of what will work as the man in the moon.'

How to get voice-over work

You need to target radio stations who have their own commercial production facility, studios who make them for stations that don't, and video production companies who need voice-overs to narrate the films they make. Forget advertising agencies; they're usually only interested in the well-known names for big budget campaigns. You may try to interest an agent in representing you, but as we've already learnt, they may want only very experienced people on their books, unless you have something unique to offer. You may find suitable agents under 'Theatrical and Variety Agents' in *Yellow Pages*, or buy a copy of the **Artists and Agents Handbook** (Richmond House Publishing, 0171 437 9556). If you're going to sell yourself direct, a spell at the library copying numbers and addresses from all the *Yellow Pages* directories in your region should pay off. Look up contacts under 'Audio-Visual Services', 'Recording Services – Sound', 'TV Film and Video Production Services' and 'Video Services'. Call first to check if it's worth sending a cassette; find out who does the hiring, and check the spelling of the name.

If you're also looking for work as a radio presenter, the tape you make will be completely different from the cassettes you send round to the radio stations. Think what you're best at, and put it first on the tape. If you're hot at impressions, include an ad with three or four characters all played by you. Follow this with a few straight reads. If you have a deep, resonant voice, start your tape with a few reads which show you off to your best. Follow this with something different to display your flexibility.

If you haven't done much, or any, voice work, you have a choice:

■ Commercials and extracts from commentaries which sound as if they could be real. In other words, make up names of shops and services which you could have voiced for someone on the other side of the country – they're not going to know. If your tape is going to someone in Bournemouth, make up addresses in Preston. It may be a cheat, but why not give the impression you're an established voice-over in another region?

■ Comedy 'spoof' commercials which are obviously made up, but still show your voice talent to the full. Make the whole tape a concept, with genuinely funny gags which the recipient will appreciate. Give them a reason for listening to the whole of your tape, and they'll remember you. (Top UK voice Mike Hurley has been making these sorts of tapes for years, and when a studio receives one of his new hilarious showtapes in the post, it's a major event.)

When you are happy with your tape, duplicate it on to quality chrome cassettes (duplicating companies will charge about 60p for a ten-minute copy) and package it up professionally. This means neat labels on the cassette (ideally printed) and a concise covering letter folded inside the package. Don't use a padded bag which is barely cassette-size; paperwork looks terrible wrapped tightly round a tape. A mailer which takes A4 folded once will be fine. Type the label – the recipient may actually be the one to open your package and first impressions count!

Three or four days after mailing the tape, call up your contact and ask if the tape has been heard yet. Ask if there are any projects coming up or unbooked voice-over sessions on which you could help out. Remember, radio stations do tend to book up their weekly- or twice-weekly sessions months in advance, so don't be too put off if you call in September and are given a date after Christmas.

A good tip is to pretend that you are 'in the area' next week, so could 'pop in' to voice a few scripts. Most commercial producers will feel guilty offering only a few paid scripts for a day's travelling, so if you give the impression you're working in their region anyway, they may give you a try if they like your cassette. Of course, you may then have to travel a hundred miles just for £30, but actually *meeting* people can really pay off when it comes to securing future work.

Female voice-overs

Listen to radio and television and you'll hear a majority of male voices. For whatever reason, female voice-overs are relatively scarce. However, a really good female voice can earn a good deal of money, and the current lack of competition is an advantage. Of course, you may get landed with the stereotypical 'housewife over the garden fence' or 'vamp in the night-club' parts, but if you've a clear, pleasant voice and possess all the skills mentioned earlier, you'll also be well placed to do straight commercials or commentaries.

Judith Franklin is a presenter and voice-over who works in the Midlands and North on a variety of different projects, from narrating 'talking books' to voicing radio station commercials. She is also the presenter of the network daytime TV series *Gardeners' Diary*. 'There's always been a problem for women voice-overs. When I am called to do a session with a male voice-over at a radio station, once we have done our recordings together I am shown the door while the male presenter stays on to voice-over a pile of other commercials. For some reason the advertising industry still has this idea that the male voice is more authoritative. If only radio commercials were planned and written with as much care as TV ads, maybe more scripts could be put together with women in mind.'

So what is Judith's advice for people who want to get started in voice-over work? 'Some kind of audition tape is important but the clearest, most attractive voice in the world won't guarantee a booking. Studio producers are very worried that anybody new will use up a lot of their valuable time just being shown the ropes. You've somehow got to persuade them that you are more experienced than you really are to put their minds at rest. Practise at home with dummy scripts, use an accurate watch to fit the required number of words into exactly thirty seconds, read the scripts in different styles and accents... All these things are essential skills which you should master before you start phoning round to be booked.'

Contactability

Quite often, voice work has to be recorded at the very last minute. If an agency or recording studio want you, they have to be able to contact you fast. If they can't get you, or if it's a hassle, they may go elsewhere.

A mobile telephone is invaluable for a working voice-over who spends his or her life travelling between studios (and is tax deductible if you're a freelance). If you can't afford this, leave numbers on your answering machine (a device which is essential for *all* broadcasters) where you can be contacted at any time in the day.

When buying an answering machine, choose one with remote access which will play back messages down the line to you. Phoning your machine every few hours to check for messages is a far cheaper option than employing a telephone answering service, which probably wouldn't be able to contact you fast enough anyway if you didn't have a mobile.

By the way, if you have a mobile phone, don't forget to switch it off during any session; it may give the impression that you're in demand when it rings, but Sod's law states that it will always ring during a really good take!

CHAPTER 14
USING YOUR PERSONALITY

WHERE DOES YOUR personality come from? Your genetic inheritance, or your upbringing and experience of life? I don't really know, but I do realise how difficult it is to put it across on the air. I have worked with many presenters who are humorous, knowledgeable people off-air, but who seem mindless, bland anybodies on radio or television.

It's such a shame. Some people are so forthright about their views on world news in their own sitting rooms, love spreading the latest gossip in the canteen, are the life and soul of the party – then go on-air to present a radio show with a succession of *'Well, there you go'*, *'That was, this is ...'*-type links.

I'll say this again: you have to give listeners and viewers a *reason* for switching onto your programme. Say what you *really* feel about a subject, don't just read a newspaper cutting or 'what's on' without giving a punchline or comment. Don't be embarrassed – you win some, you lose some, but if you don't try, you won't succeed. If you want to show you're different from the sea of faceless presenters, you have to let your true personality shine through.

Even broadcasters who are tightly scripted have to be aware of the personality they transmit. No matter how well you think you are reading the stories, it will be obvious to the viewers or listeners whether you are an intelligent, well-informed individual with a good understanding of what you're saying, or whether you are merely reading words, smiling in the right places but only really looking forward to a drink in the club afterwards.

You can't be someone you're not, but you can develop your own confidence, vocabulary skills, knowledge of current affairs and observational powers, and learn how to express yourself more efficiently.

Confidence

Confidence comes from ego-building. When you're alone, look in the mirror and say:

> 'I have opinions which the world wants to hear.'
> 'I am informed and interesting.'
> 'I am humorous and good to know.'

It's worth noting the old theatrical three-liner, which is meant to give thespians waiting in the wings the confidence to give a killer performance when it's their turn to step onto the stage. It goes: '*I am beautiful*', '*I know a secret*', and '*Everybody loves me*'. Try this before the red light comes on in the studio, or before you're announced on stage; it really can work wonders if you are nervous.

If someone says, 'You did a good programme today,' don't be hypercritical and snap back, 'No, it was rubbish.' Accept the compliment and make sure that the next programme is up to the same standard. If people say the opposite, sort out the reason why you messed up, but don't dwell on mistakes, you can't turn back time.

Forget the saying, '*You're only as good as your last programme.*' If a live programme really *was* a disaster, *never* refer back to it on the subsequent show. Tell yourself that no one actually listened to or watched the duff programme, or else you'll be over-anxious and it will ruin your future performance. In reality, disasters, particularly technical ones, are seldom remarked upon by the public or the press.

There are plenty of tricks you can play on yourself to improve your confidence, down to 'whistling a happy tune', but at the end of the day that genuine deep-down satisfaction will only come if you know you're doing your job well and can cope with the unexpected. After a few months' experience, there will come a day when you will walk out of a studio and think to yourself, '*That was a hell of a good programme, I was really on the ball, I coped with those callers well, my ad-libbed introduction to that final item was the business . . . Boy, I'm good!*' And you'll really mean it. There is nothing to beat the inner satisfaction of having done a job professionally and successfully. This feeling, added to the adrenalin high of presenting on TV and radio, makes all the struggle worthwhile.

Humour and sensitivity

I've put these two together, because the two are linked. You can't be funny unless you're sensitive to the mood and expectations of your audience. Follow a stand-up comic on tour and watch how the act is adapted to suit the differing audiences and types of venues. The difficulty with humour on radio and TV is that you can't actually see the audience; you don't know if they're laughing or switching you off.

On TV, you'll find most of the humour has been pre-written and honed to blandness. Watch any regional TV news programme and the once funny link into the weather forecaster has usually been transformed into a play on an old pun, delivered without any spark after half-a-dozen rehearsals. The best humour comes as an ad-lib, a natural and witty retort to something that has just happened. On a live TV show, of course, your ad-lib may eat up valuable seconds of the air time, so listen in your earpiece; the director normally updates everyone regularly to say whether the show is under- or over-running. One of the dangers of ad-libbing is that you may say something that's funny to some, but offensive to others. Take a little time to think it over before committing yourself. For example, a poignant piece about a hit and run incident might include a reconstruction including a shot from inside the car which shows two fluffy dice. You have the world's best gag about fluffy dice on the tip of your tongue . . . Do you use it, coming out of that particular film? I think you get my drift. Once again, your sensitivity is important.

On both radio and TV, you should keep in the back of your mind one person who is listening or watching you: one person who represents your station's ideal audience. This will help you not to slip into pluralisms, such as 'All of you are advised . . .' when it should be the more personable 'You are advised . . .' You can also test your humour on your personal mental watchdog. Some broadcasters keep a real person, such as their mother or a good friend, in mind. This imaginary person can change of course; when I'm broadcasting on JFM, an upmarket jazz and blues station, I imagine I am talking to a smart, successful business person, aged about 35, who drives a Mercedes Benz. For programmes on BBC local radio, I imagine my listener is someone a little older, an honest, friendly, hard-working person who is fiercely proud of the region in which he lives. Whoever your imaginary listener or viewer is, remember that you have to relate to both sexes; a gag which goes down well at a lads' rugby club may not be so warmly received at a meeting of the WRVS. It's down to sensitivity again.

Vocabulary skills

Read a quality newspaper, listen to news and discussion programmes on a good speech radio station and look up words which you don't know or aren't sure about. Write them in a 'new word' notebook and review it every week. Don't bother learning random 'long' words from a dictionary; most words you will never need. Be sure you know the context in which you can use these new words as well as their pure meaning – don't make a fool of yourself like Mrs Malaprop in *The Rivals*.

Current affairs and observational powers

By current affairs, I don't mean merely memorising the headlines in the daily papers. If you're a local radio presenter, keep up-to-date with the important issues in the area you cover. Look at national and local stories in some depth.

Take care with the stories you choose to comment on; you don't want to bore your listeners with observations such as '*Oh, isn't it awful about that motorcyclist who was knocked down last night?*' New shopping developments, roads, transport, important visitors to the city, local heroes, local charity news, interesting events and happenings – your reactions to all or any of these must be original and thought-provoking, so you can produce a similar response in your audience.

Take clippings from the national and local papers and free-sheets and file them in a folder for use during the week. Keep a notebook with you and write down topical or timely observations or jokes. Anything interesting you say, or that somebody says to you; anything you encounter during the day that makes you think '*That's interesting/ funny / stupid / outrageous*' write it in the book, or else you'll forget it. Just a few words should remind you of the whole story when you're next on-air.

Anecdotes and observations that are well presented with a punch-line (serious or witty) distinguish a professional, top-line presenter from a run-of-the-mill disc jockey.

Express yourself

See how well you can express yourself in this exercise.

As in the well-known BBC radio panel game *Just a Minute*, speak aloud (into a tape machine) for one minute on the subjects listed below. Don't be embarrassed – this is very serious training for any broadcaster who wants to be a true professional, a person who can intelligently ad-lib themselves out of any situation. Here we go, and don't forget – no repetition, hesitation or deviation!

- The railway network today
- Household chores
- Telling youngsters the facts of life
- Remote controls
- Beach holidays
- Early marriages
- Door-to-door salespeople
- Life after death
- Gold credit cards

CHAPTER 15

PROMOTING YOURSELF

A S A WORKING PRESENTER, you must strive, at all times, to keep your profile high. Obviously you will want to broadcast as much as possible, but there are plenty of other ways to promote yourself, not just to fuel your ego, but to ensure that your standing against other, rival presenters does not drop and that supplementary jobs are regularly offered to you.

Even if you are a staff presenter or have a long contract, in the competitive, fragile world of broadcasting you need as much kudos, publicity and money you can get. Here are some tactics that you might like to try:

☐ Send 'press releases' about yourself to the press. Daily 'diary'-type pages in local papers are usually desperate for stories. Send them a few paragraphs about anything interesting that has happened to you, or that *could* (feasibly) have happened to you. Think of the sorts of stories the paper prints about media people; what story would they want to believe? What image do you want to project?

If you are the sort of person who believes everything you read in black and white must be true, you may be shocked at my implication that you should feed a few white lies into your press release to perk it up. Believe me, there are plenty of journalists working on the lighter features and gossip columns who not only don't have the time to check the information you are feeding them, but don't care if you have faxed them a load of porky pies. As long as the stuff sounds believable and'll make good reading, they'll print it.

☑ Contact local papers to see if they would be interested in your writing a regular column for them. You could not only get your photo in a weekly paper, but also get paid for telling the world your views.

☑ Take part in charity events that attract media coverage. On the day, stay close to any celebrities present; you may end up pictured next to them in the press.

☑ Keep a profile in the *trade* press by informing them of your own opinions on developments in the industry; you may find your way on to the Letters Page, at least. Magazines like *Broadcast*, *Stage and Television Today* and *Radio Week* are all useful publications to contact.

☑ Always have copies of up-to-date colour and black and white photographs ready to send to the press. Put sticky labels on the back, with your name and telephone numbers.

☑ Build up a network of contacts around the industry. Swap telephone numbers at the end of each job or shoot and call useful contacts every so often – they may have good leads for future work.

☑ Get on the mailing lists of local theatres for review tickets. It's often possible to make contact with writers from the showbusiness press at First Nights.

☑ Always be courteous to everyone – your own team and, of course, the public, no matter how rushed you are. Don't ruin your on-air image when you're off-air. Bad reputations spread fast, and that researcher you were rude to could be your producer next year!

Personal appearances

Turning up at a public event is an important part of a presenter's life, but it doesn't always go to plan. Let's look at a nightmare scenario. The memo from your promotions department reads like this:

> *You have been booked to make a half-hour appearance at the Didshot Carnival, this Saturday the 28th. Arriving at 2 pm, you will be met by Tom Phillips at the gate who will show you to your car park space and personal dressing room. Your duties will be to open the Carnival at 2.30 pm and then tour the stalls for half an hour maximum. A public address system will be provided and you will have twenty sweatshirts to give away. Fee £100.*

I've heard it all before. On the day, nobody at the gate knows who or where Tom Phillips is, so you have to pay to park in the public car park and walk half a mile through a muddy field to the site. You eventually find someone in charge, only to discover that you have to share your 'personal dressing room' with fifteen screaming drum majorettes and a fire-eating act who stinks of paraffin. The 'public address system' turns out to be a cheap microphone plugged into an even cheaper amplifier balanced on a trestle table, which distorts so badly that you have to resort to shouting. The sweatshirts you have been promised never arrive, and you are persuaded by the organisers to draw the raffle, which means you have to hang around until 4.30 pm, trying to make polite conversation with the vicar's wife and enduring yet another police dog display and brass band concert in the arena. To add insult to injury, you eventually find out that there was a typing error on the memo, and your fee is actually only £10. . .

Not all personal appearances are as bad as this, but they can get close. The important thing on the day is to keep looking professional and keep smiling. You have the reputation of your radio or TV station to think of as well as your own.

To prevent a situation like the above, never trust anybody! Call the organisers personally and confirm the details in case your promotions department have missed anything. Check that they have received your photographs and posters to display before the event and check the times that you'll be needed. Confirm the equipment that you want on the day. Tell them that you have another engagement after theirs, and you have to get away – even if you haven't. On the day, be prepared! Always carry a spare bag of promotional goods in your car.

If you're nervous about what to say at a public function, use this tried and tested formula:

- ☑ Present yourself to the public as you do in your radio or TV programme. Keep in character.
- ☑ Research the event or location. Get the brochure or programme well in advance.
- ☑ Start your speech with a few snappy gags relating to your radio or TV show. This will help people who aren't familiar with your programme to identify who you are and where you come from.
- ☑ Follow with a few Thank you's to the people who have done all the hard work in making the event possible. Memorise the important names. This always goes down well.
- ☑ Now tell people what is on offer at the fête / carnival / exhibition, making gags as appropriate.
- ☑ Don't be afraid to involve others. Persuading the May Queen to cut the ribbon always gets an 'aah'.

☑ Finally, thank the people for listening or watching your programme and officially open the event.

☑ Keep it short . . . always leave them wanting more!

Remember, you are an outsider at a community event. Be courteous at all times, maintain your professionalism and respect the wishes of the organisers – even if they force you to sit through yet *another* trampoline display. . .

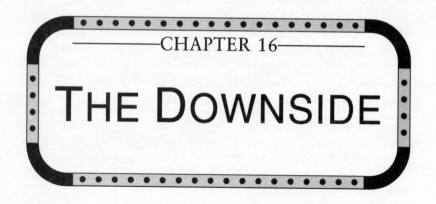

CHAPTER 16

THE DOWNSIDE

*A*S *WITH ANY JOB*, you have to take the rough with the smooth. It's not always enjoyable or even pleasant working in broadcasting. The industry has gone through turmoil in recent years, particularly television; more and more TV stations are being run by accountants, rather than programme makers. Viewing figures and profit and loss accounts are now considered more important than production values: factual and current affairs programmes which traditionally do not attract peak audiences are being squeezed for resources and are also being squeezed out of prime-time slots, to make way for mass-market entertainment shows and soaps. Essential in-house production departments like news cutting and videotape libraries have been cut back, so life is now even more frustrating for the people who have to create the shows which make the money. Many internal training schemes are much less thorough than they used to be, or have been scrapped altogether, so newcomers have to learn their skills at external colleges, often at their own expense.

So how will this affect you, the potential presenter or on-screen reporter? As well as having to accept lower initial fees until your popularity proves itself, you'll find yourself working much harder. Where, say, a ten-minute documentary item used to take two shooting days to make, including an overnight stay, you could find that the budget has cut this down to one very, very long day with hours of travelling at both ends. You may be asked to do more than simply present; understaffed programmes often desperately need another person to help set up stories, view tapes or recce locations.

Another result of TV cutbacks is the ever-shortening contract. Many freelance presenters and reporters are finding that the usual two- or one-year contract is being replaced by a six-month or even a three-month contract. This allows television companies and production houses more flexibility to change things around (i.e. fire you) if things get tough. This situation means that during the last month of your contract you are so busy chasing other opportunities, or trying to get confirmation of a contract renewal, that your work may suffer.

If this insecurity were not bad enough, you will find it difficult to plan holidays or even weekends away. Programme-making is an uncertain business. Television filming is notoriously unpredictable, and you may be asked to come in again on your day off to refilm something because of one of many reasons: a camera fault, a continuity error or even a missing page of the script left on an office photocopier.

Even if you can put up with all this with a cheerful smile, you may be unlucky enough to encounter some of the nastier types of media people, who have become so twisted and bitter by their circumstances that they take things out on you. A thick skin is one of many things you may have to develop in your new career in broadcasting.

A good example of how unglamorous television work can be is overseas filming, which is perceived as wildly exciting. I have regularly filmed abroad for various programmes and I can assure you, it is no free holiday! Even though your location may be exotic, you will be under extreme pressure to come up with good shots for your report or programme, and working in a strange land with possible language problems adds to stress levels.

Overseas filming means even longer hours (in TV they call this 'unusual hours') and staying in seedy hotels if the budget is low. There will probably be a lot of travelling, usually driving at breakneck speed against the clock so as not to miss the next location rendezvous. (Now you know why media people pay over the odds for motoring insurance.)

Time is the greatest enemy for a crew filming on location. Hiring a basic crew of camera operator, sound recordist, electrician and presenter/reporter will not give the programme producer much change out of £1,500 per day. This doesn't take into account facility fees (paying the people who own the locations), equipment hire, travel and hotel bills . . . it all mounts up. If a TV programme has three shooting days in its budget, the crew are under immense pressure not to exceed this. The high spirits at the start of the day can rapidly degenerate into extreme depression and shouting matches if time (or simply daylight) runs out.

You'll have to learn to get on with new people very fast, filming on the road. Then the camera operator loses interest in the shoot, the hand-held light blows and the electrician admits he's forgotten the spares . . . and it's virtually a full-blown fist fight before there's even a shot 'in the can'.

But what about your general lifestyle? How will this change when you join the broadcasting industry? The uncertainty of it all can play havoc with your personal life. You may have to pull out of a dinner party at the last minute because you have to fill in for a sick presenter, or haven't managed to get that piece finished in time. You may spend hours up in the loft looking for records or videotape rushes you desperately need the next day, while friends pop in for a drink and leave again without even seeing you. You may be under the bedclothes with a torch desperately scribbling scripts for your next programme or reading press cuttings while your partner is trying to get you interested in something slightly more erotic. . .

It's important for presenters to act as normally as possible outside the studio, or they will find their whole life distorted and disturbed. People in supermarkets will stare in your direction and whisper to each other. Are they talking about you, or discussing whether the cauliflowers behind you are a good buy this week? If people look meaningfully at you, smile back and get on with whatever you are doing.

You will sometimes have to cope with straight confrontations: *'Aren't you the bloke off the telly?'* It never pays in life to be rude to anyone, and especially so here. Even if you're in a hurry, treat your public with respect – after all, they indirectly pay your wages. Just remind them of your name, channel, thank them for watching your programme and move on.

Let's examine a few of the myths perpetuated by members of the public, when they say to you: *'It must be wonderful to work in radio or telly, because . . .'*

MYTH NO. 1: 'YOU MEET ALL THE STARS!' You could be working with, or have occasion to interview, quite a few famous and respected people. It might give you a buzz at first to meet someone you've admired for years, but it's no big deal, honestly. And 'stars' often present the most difficulties as far as being co-operative goes.

MYTH NO. 2: 'I BET YOU GO TO PARTIES EVERY NIGHT!' When do we *ever* get *time* to go to all these parties we're alleged to go to? Jobs and problems eat up every spare minute. Even meals are more often than not curled-up sandwiches brought into your meeting, editing booth or recording studio.

MYTH NO. 3: 'YOU MUST HAVE GIRLS / FELLAS AFTER YOU ALL THE TIME!' It's true it's easier to break the ice with someone of the opposite sex because you're in broadcasting. For some reason the job impresses more than announcing that you are the North East rep for a bathroom cabinet furniture company (left-handed knob division). I wonder why? However, again, when would you find the *time* to follow up all the possible leads of friendship or romance? The people who write adoringly to DJs or presenters tend to be two vouchers short of a pop-up toaster anyway. I've found the best friends and lovers are those who are completely indifferent to your 'fame'.

MYTH NO. 4: 'YOUR WIFE / GIRLFRIEND / HUSBAND / BOYFRIEND MUST BE *SO* PROUD OF YOU!' I'm sure she'd tell me, if I ever saw her. A lot of 'broadcasting' relationships suffer huge strains because of the irregular working patterns.

MYTH NO. 5 'YOUR PARENTS MUST BE *SO* PROUD OF YOU!' Parents may well be a little chuffed if they live in your transmission area. But to most people who grew up before the boom in mass broadcasting, earning real money just for saying a few words into a microphone or to a camera is either a joke, a con, or both. If only broadcasting were respectable...

CHAPTER 17

PLANNING FOR THE FUTURE

M*ANY RADIO AND TV* presenters have a limited 'shelf life'. Their radio station may change to a new 'sound' and their style may not suit it, or on TV their face may not fit any more. Presenters get older, more set in their ways, unable or unwilling to change or to move to find work. Younger, more adaptable stars appear on the horizon.

So how does a presenter stay on top? Over the years, Steve Penk has seen the ratings of his breakfast show on Key 103 in Greater Manchester rise, and he has been offered more and more TV work as well. Does he not worry that the bubble may eventually burst?

'Like anybody with a family to support, I'm concerned about future regular employment, but I'm also very aware that presenters must never, *ever*, become complacent, especially if they have good audience ratings under their belt. What goes up, can come down. I am forever making a conscious effort to monitor what my audience wants, and I'm quite willing to drop mannerisms, catchphrases or whole features if they're getting tired and need updating. Over the last few years, for example, I've become infamous in the area for my wind-up phone calls, an idea which is being adapted for a network TV show. The success of this will continue for some time to come, I'm sure, but I'm very conscious of the fact that I could be saddled with being thought of only as "Mr Wind-Up", which will do me no good if the idea loses popularity.

'My advice to all your readers is: work very, very hard as soon as you get a break on-air and don't be a prima-donna – after all, it is not your station.'

It's very important for you to realise that a break on-air doesn't put you on the gravy train for life, and you should always keep in mind other long-term broadcasting opportunities so that you don't suddenly find yourself on the sad and long roll-call of the has-beens. This is why any experience in news reporting or current affairs programmes is always a good investment. If you are solid and reliable, station bosses would have little reason to discontinue your contract just because you are 'out of vogue', or 'looking too old'. Indeed, your age may add to your authority! Obviously, there are many presenter-type jobs that could financially keep your head above water if you were suddenly 'let go'. These might include voice-over work or corporate video presentation.

Multi-skilling

Always remember: the more skills you can offer, the more likely it is that you will stay in employment. The power of the various broadcasting unions has decreased considerably over the last ten years in the UK, and this period has seen both employer and employee taking advantage of 'multi-skilling'. For example, years ago, a television sound recordist could have caused a walkout if he as much as moved an electrician's light on location. These days, most television stations have trained sound people to rig lights as part of their jobs, and allow electricians (or 'sparks') to train as sound recordists.

As a presenter, you too must always look out for jobs you can take on when you fall out of favour as on-air talent. Ask questions of others; get involved; learn. Your job will be more satisfying if you understand why the camera operator is putting a certain filter over the lens or why the director has decided to reshoot a scene in a different way – you'll get an insight into broadcasting jobs that you may have a genuine flair for in years to come.

I first got into the multi-skilling way of thinking when I was working for a television newsroom where there were five editing suites, with only three editors between them. It was frustrating waiting for your turn, with freshly shot video tapes in hand and the clock ticking away towards the deadline. So I taught myself how to work the equipment, first using it to view and log my material and then to perform simple edits. A friendly VT editor, in his spare time, showed me what all the buttons did, and editing has proved to be another valuable skill.

Today, I sell myself as a producer, director, scriptwriter, media tutor, and journalist as well as voice-over, radio presenter, and television presenter. Some say I have made myself a 'Jack of all trades', but I'm always in work and enjoy a great variety of jobs – so why not?

Going freelance

Once upon a time, in the days of a highly unionised and overstaffed industry, broadcasters virtually all had jobs on the staff and could relax, secure in the knowledge that each month little pieces of paper called 'pay slips' would appear in the internal mail. These days have gone. We are now, like it or not, living in the age of the freelance.

Most of the broadcasting jobs you see advertised these days will not be for staff positions, but will offer a contract arrangement. This may be for a period of weeks, months or years, but it gives the employer flexibility; they don't have to pay you a bean after the contract expires. Look at it from their point of view: if they ask you to present an eight-week TV series with a four-week run-up time, why give you a six-month contract when nobody knows if there is to be a further series afterwards? If you are hired as a freelance, it also means that the company doesn't have to worry about paying your National Insurance and pension contributions and, in some cases, insuring you for driving the company's vehicles. Your contract may pay you per programme you work on, or pay you over a period. '*What's this got to do with me?*' you're asking. Well, it's almost certain that your first real paid work for a radio or TV station will be on a short contract so management can see if you have the potential for a longer-term future. You will most likely start life as a freelance. You *may* then get the choice of a staff post or a freelance contract, although nowadays it's more often Hobson's Choice: the freelance option. So keep your wits about you. I regularly hear of presenters who signed up for a poor contract in their hungry, early days, only to regret it when they had 'made it'. Be aware of your rights and don't make a rash decision just to get on air!

ADVANTAGES OF BEING ON STAFF

■ Security. You may still be thrown out if they suddenly decide they don't like you or the company goes bust, but your staff status should ensure that you will be eligible for some kind of compensation, even if you have to fight for it.

■ You don't have to worry about sorting out National Health or pension contributions, and because income tax is deducted before you get your hands on your pay packet, there is no temptation to spend what isn't yours.

DISADVANTAGES OF BEING ON STAFF

■ Let's say your contract is as a regional presenter or reporter for two years and you are given the going rate for that job. What if you are asked during this period to front a major network programme made by your company, a job which would normally command a much higher rate? Usually it's tough luck.

■ As a staff person, you will have to take the rough with the smooth; the company will find work for you to do, even if you don't like it. If you're told to present an overnight radio show or become a reporter at an outpost newsroom away from the main production centre, you'll have to do it.

ADVANTAGES OF BEING FREELANCE

■ Flexibility and variety. You may never know what you're doing from day to day.

■ You may be able to earn more. Freelance rates are generally higher than the equivalent staff salaries. This is because you have to bear all your own overheads – phone, car, lighting, pension contributions, etc. What's more, you can renegotiate every time you're booked.

■ Reach for the moon. The sky's the limit. You can pitch for work with a list of different companies, think up new money-making schemes, get involved with speculative productions. All this is open to you if you are not tied to one company, and are prepared to travel.

DISADVANTAGES OF BEING FREELANCE

■ Accounts and paperwork. This can really get you down. You have to log and file away all your business-related receipts, send out invoices and reminders (eventually legal letters when companies don't shell out), and work out the VAT returns if you are registered. Currently you have to be registered if your turnover is £45,000 or more per year. Then there are the end-of-year tax returns. You will have to keep a business mileage book in your car and use it to log all your business travel. Dates, locations and mileage between each job will need to be recorded. The tax people may need to see this when you claim business travel in your tax return.

■ Irregular work. When things are getting slack and you book a holiday, you can bet that a nice fat job is suddenly offered to you in the very period you have booked for. Staff people can usually plan their holiday breaks . . . and enjoy them. Luxury. In practice, many freelances don't take holidays at all some years, because they are constantly touting for work, or working flat out on rush jobs.

■ No work. Nothing is guaranteed, and even a contract may be riddled with legal loopholes rendering it useless if they don't want you anymore. Times may get hard, work may dry up, and you'll have to survive somehow.

■ Being constantly on the lookout for new employment opportunities. You have to scour the trade press, badger people in corridors – the stress is often immense and, if you have a family to support, the lack of security can be a real problem.

If you are in full-time employment, *don't* go freelance until you are certain that you are going to secure enough work for at least the next six months. In other words, you need a contract that will give you a basic guaranteed income until you make the contacts to earn you a good amount of 'one-off' work like commercial voice-over sessions, corporate video writing or presentation or whatever you feel you can do that other people will pay you money for.

ACCOUNTANTS Find a good accountant: one who really understands your type of work and knows the sorts of things broadcasters can claim against tax. As a brief guide, here's a list of goods and services you can tell your accountant you've purchased over the financial year which should be tax deductible:

■ materials you need for your work: video and audio cassettes, tape boxes, etc.
■ secretarial services
■ make-up and hairdressing bills
■ clothing, if specially required for your work
■ laundry and dry-cleaning of your professional clothing
■ travelling expenses when going to auditions and interviews
■ subscriptions to trade unions and relevant professional organisations: BECTU, Equity, Musicians' Union, etc – any of the organisations listed in Factfile 2
■ stationery and postal charges
■ subscriptions to professional and trade magazines
■ publicity photographs and advertising
■ voice training, elocution lessons, etc
■ legal fees for bad debt recovery
■ accountancy fees
■ agent's fees and commissions

The business costs of using your home, phone and car are tax deductible. Large items you've bought for your business use, like a car, recording equipment, word processor, musical instruments if you write jingles, etc, are called 'Capital Expenses'. A proportion of their costs can be written off each year. Ask your accountant for more details on all this.

AGENTS   An agent is someone who represents you, and takes bookings on your behalf for a percentage of the fee. They should send out your pictures and tapes to the right organisations, and be on the ball when any new job presents itself. You don't always need an agent, however, and a bad one may give you false hope that a lot of work is 'coming round the corner', while you sit at home waiting for the phone to ring.

The advantage of having a good agent on your side is that they will have access to a lot of contacts, and tend to know of auditions coming up which haven't been advertised. When there's a 'bite', they can usually negotiate a higher rate, and sort out all the contract work surrounding things like repeat fees.

Here's some advice if you do decide to work with an agent:

- ☑ Find one who understands your work and can sell for you. For example, if you specialise in voice-overs and entertainment work, why be represented by an agency that mainly deals with drama work?
- ☑ Make sure your agent will invoice the clients and chase all fees. Some agencies ask *you* to invoice people and send them the commission when you receive the fee.
- ☑ Sort out who pays for publicity pictures, your inserts in *Spotlight* and other directories, video and audio cassettes, postage on mailshots, and so on. Sometimes agent and performer go 50/50 on these things; but usually you pay for everything bar the postage.

When you contact an agency, you must show promise and professionalism. An agent won't usually touch you if you haven't had any experience at all, so you'll probably have to make a start on your own. However, if you're an ambitious newcomer, an appointment with an agent may well give you some invaluable pointers, even if you don't get invited onto their books.

THE TRAINING COURSES

IF YOU FIND YOU are coming up against closed doors in broadcasting because of your lack of experience and knowledge, it is quite natural to want to embark on a training course to gain more credibility. However, there is a school of thought in broadcasting that there is no substitute for the University of Life. Certainly some television news editors would prefer to hire a journalist with reporting experience on a newspaper or radio station in addition to any relevant qualification achieved, rather than an applicant who had simply completed a wholly academic training course.

The best form of training should include both the theoretical and practical aspects of the job in as real a situation as possible, that is, within a working broadcasting environment. No lecture theatre or mocked-up studio set can prepare you for the unique intensities and pressures associated with on-air work. If you are choosing a media training course, look for two important pointers: that the people training you have had some actual broadcasting experience, and that the college or university has strong links with local radio and TV stations. It is very important that your course should include work experience in a genuine broadcasting environment. Some colleges even produce radio and TV programmes for their local radio or TV station.

The **University College Admissions Service** (01242 222444) can send you their latest *UCAS Handbook*, which includes many courses on media studies, broadcasting and journalism. For postgraduate studies, Hobsons (01223 354551) publish a guide called ***Graduate Studies.***

The **National Film and Television School** (01494 671234) is an educational charity which has its own studios. Based in Beaconsfield,

Buckinghamshire, it offers three-year full-time courses in writing, directing and production. The course fees are £2,260 per year (at time of publication) for UK residents. Only around fifty students are accepted each year, and applicants have to prove that they have the talent and enthusiasm to be successful in the industry.

The **British Film Institute** (0171 636 3289) has an education department which offers a guide on film and video courses, *Media Courses in the UK*; it costs £8.95. The **National Association for Higher Education in Film and Video** (0171 836 9642) can provide information on all training courses offering study of film, video or TV at higher education level.

The **BBC** regularly recruits small numbers of trainees for specific job categories: either at school-leaver level for technical or administration jobs, or at graduate level for studio manager, television production and news trainee places. There is also a general trainee category. The regional news trainee scheme offers training at one of the BBC's provincial news centres. Most traineeships last one year with *no guaranteed employment* at the end of this time. Pay varies: news trainees, for example, receive around £1,000 per month. Details of the BBC's traineeships can be obtained from BBC Recruitment Services, PO Box 7000, London W12 7ZY (0181 752 5252).

Most of the larger ITV companies have some sort of internal training scheme for a few new journalists and directors each year and the **ITV Association** in London (0171 843 8000) offers advice and guidance on training and runs various courses including one aimed at new presenters.

Professional bodies like the **Royal Television Society** (0171 430 1000) can also help in choosing a training course. There is a free careers pack available from **Skillsett**, 60 Charlotte Street, London W1P 2AX (0171 927 8585), an industry training operation aimed at newcomers to broadcasting. **Networking** (0113 242 8646) is an organisation set up in Leeds particularly for women who want to work in video or TV. They publish a newsletter and contacts lists. There is also the **Women's Audio Visual Education Scheme**, 4 Wild Court, London WC2B 5AU (0171 430 1076), which trains women in TV and radio work.

Performance skills

But what if you need to enhance pure performance skills? A course in scriptwriting and reporting would not be suitable if your goal is to front a game show or children's entertainment programme. A course at a theatre school might provide a better background for you. You will find that some courses will include voice training and presentation as well as drama skills.

A list of courses is in *Spotlight Contacts*, published each October (0171 437 7631) and the Irish version is the *Stagecast Directory*, published in Monkstown, Dublin (010 353 1 280 8968). Both these books also list agents and other media contacts.

Or why not find out more by contacting theatre schools direct? You might discover just the course you want to improve your performance talents. Here is a selection:

- The **Academy of Live and Recorded Arts**, Royal Victoria Patriotic Building, Trinity Road, London SW18 3SX (0181 870 6475)
- **Ackerley Studios of Speech and Drama**, Crane Studios, Harbour Street, Liverpool L1 3DZ (0151 709 5995)
- **Alternative to Drama School**, 20 Waldegrave Road, London SE19 2AJ (0181 653 7854)
- **Bristol Old Vic Theatre School**, 1 Downside Road, Bristol BS8 2XF (0117 973 3535)
- **Central School of Speech and Drama**, Embassy Theatre, Eton Avenue, London NW3 3HY (0181 772 8183)
- **Manchester Metropolitan University**, School of Theatre, The Capitol Building, School Lane, Didsbury, Manchester M20 0HT (0161 247 2000, ext. 7123)
- **Northern Theatre School of Performing Arts**, Madeley Street, Hull HU3 2AH (0482 28627)
- **Performing Arts School**, The Dance Centre, Diggles Lane, Dublin 2, Eire (010 353 11 1784 1790)
- **Rose Bruford College of Speech and Drama**, Lamorbey Park, Sidcup, Kent DA15 9DF (0181 300 3024).

Joining a theatre company direct may pay dividends. The *Amateur Theatre Year Book* (Platform Publications, 0171 486 1732) lists many company details. Or if you feel that you relate well to young people, the **Children's Theatre Association** (Unicorn Theatre, 0171 836 3623), offers opportunities at workshops and projects as well as on the stage. The *British Alternative Theatre Directory* (Rebecca Books, 01222 378452) lists all the companies, artists, and festivals in this genre.

Don't forget to find out everything about any course before you sign up; some are expensive, so you have to be very sure that any training will really be beneficial in helping you attain your eventual goal.

News training

There are plenty of ways a potential broadcast journalist can get started. A good first point of contact is the **National Union of Journalists** (0171 278 7916) who have an excellent booklet called *Careers in Journalism*, which tells you more about training and the career structure of the industry. A very useful organisation is the **National Council for the Training of Journalists (NCTJ)** (01279 430009). The NCTJ sponsor one-year, full-time education and training courses for post-A-level students and graduates at fifteen colleges around the country. All courses provide a route into a career in print and broadcast journalism. They also sell training videos and a distance-learning pack. The Periodicals Training Council run courses for newcomers in magazine work. Call them up and ask for details (0171 836 8798).

More relevant to students who know that their career is going to be focused on radio and television, is an organisation called the **National Council for the Training of Broadcast Journalism** (0181 940 0694). The NCTBJ is made up of representatives from all areas of the radio and television industry, the NUJ and colleges which offer relevant courses. The Council's role is to advise and co-operate with the colleges to ensure that industry standards of training are maintained, in courses ranging from part-time radio training modules through one-year postgraduate diploma courses to a three-year BA degree. The following are the NCTBJ recognised courses at the time of publication; as with all the contacts in this book, you're welcome to get further information direct:

- **City University**, Graduate Centre of Journalism, St John Street, London EC1V 0HB (0171 477 8229)
- **Darlington College of Technology**, Cleveland Avenue, Darlington, Co. Durham DL3 7BB (01325 486643)
- **Falmouth School of Art and Design**, Woodlane, Falmouth, Cornwall TR11 4RA (0326 211077, ext. 245)
- **Highbury College of Technology**, Cosham, Portsmouth, Hants PO6 2SA (0705 383 1311)
- **The London College of Printing**, Elephant and Castle, London SE1 6SB (0171 735 8484)
- **Trinity and All Saints College**, University of Leeds, Leeds LS18 5HD (0113 258 4341)
- **University of Central England in Birmingham**, Perry Bar, Birmingham B42 2SU (0121 331 5719)
- **University of Central Lancashire**, Department of Journalism, Chandler Building, Preston PR1 2HE (01772 201201, ext. 3765)

- **University of Wales**, Centre for Journalism Studies, 69 Park Place, Cardiff CF1 3AS (01222 394069).

It must be noted that any so-called 'postgraduate' courses don't always rule out people who have no degree. Non-graduates are considered for these courses on the basis of work experience in journalism, and other qualifications gained.

If you are not looking for a full-time course, but for short-term training to top up your existing knowledge, there are many options available, and they are advertised regularly in the press. The **London Institute** (0171 725 0810), for example, holds TV journalism courses which include visits to broadcasters' newsrooms and studios. Here are some more training schools which focus on part-time or short presentation and reporting courses, also providing facilities to produce for you that all-important audio or video showtape:

- **Corporate Vision**, 14 Soho Square, London W1V 5FB (0171 734 2335)
- **Fran Morrison Broadcasting**, 2 Putney Heath Lane, London SW15 3JG (0181 788 0503)
- **Local Radio Workshops**, Interchange Studio, Dalby Street, London NW5 3NQ (0171 284 1344)
- **Media Production Facilities**, Bon Marche Buildings, Ferndale Road, London SW9 8EJ (0171 737 7152)
- **Metel Training**, 105 Boundary Street, Liverpool L5 9YT (0151 207 2281)
- **Personal Presentation Limited**, Studio 132, 222 Kensal Road, London W10 5BN (0181 968 0421)
- **Pozitiv Productions**, c/o Thames TV, Teddington Studios, Middlesex TW11 9NT (0181 614 2558 or 01734 744079)
- **Radio Tek Training**, 6 Stucley Place, London NW1 3EG (0171 284 1130).

Finally, **The Newspaper Society** has a training department which can provide information on courses available. Write to them at Whitefriars House, 6 Carmelite Street, London, EC4 0BL. Or, there is a graduate careers information book on journalism from **Central Services Unit**, Crawford House, Manchester M13 9EP (0161 273 4233).

British Actors' Equity Association (Equity)

Guild House, Upper St Martin's Lane, London WC2H 9EG
(0171 379 6000)
Conavon Court, 12 Blackfriars Street, Salford M3 5BQ
(0161 832 3183)
Transport House, 1 Cathedral Street, Cardiff (01222 397971)
65 Bath Street, Glasgow G2 2BX (0141 332 1669).

Equity has over 45,000 members who work in the entertainment industry as actors, variety and circus performers, dancers, singers, announcers and broadcasters. It was set up in 1930 by a group of high-profile actors in order to protect less well-known members of their profession from exploitation and low pay. Today, the same *raison d'être* exists and Equity constantly campaigns on behalf of its members on many fronts, from obtaining overdue monies owed to putting pressure on theatres to improve backstage facilities. Equity has agreements in these areas of entertainment: films, TV, theatre, cabaret and clubs. There are comprehensive help and advice facilities for all members, and regular publications and meetings.

There used to be a Catch-22 system – you had to have an Equity card to get any performing work, yet to obtain a card you had to prove that you had experience. The demise of the closed-shop system now means that you do not need to be a member in order to work as a performer, but the professional status that membership conveys, and the support from the union itself, can help a lot in obtaining work and in upholding your rights. There is no real advantage in joining Equity if you want a career solely in radio; they represent performers in stage, TV and film work only. However, on-air radio experience may help in your application for membership if you want to move into in-vision work.

To obtain provisional membership of Equity, you have to prove that you have a current contract for professional work in the sphere of the performing arts. However, work as a club disc jockey, theme park host or TV extra is not valid to support an application. Your application will have to be signed by two full members. Membership fees, dependent on salary, range from £32 per year to £1,200.

Professional broadcasters enjoy the benefits of joining particularly when they are booked to voice or present TV and radio commercials. As members, they are covered and protected by the standard contracts agreed with the industry, which include the complex repeat fee agreements, and so on. Although it is not *essential* for broadcasters to join Equity, it is very worthwhile angling for membership. It is considered a matter of 'professional pride' to be a member, agents will take you more seriously, and, if you are a freelance, remember that the membership fees of all work-related organisations are tax deductible.

The Royal Television Society

Holborn Hall, 100 Grays Inn Road, London WC1X 8AL
(0171 430 1000).

What began as a small group of technical enthusiasts in 1927, nine years before the first public television broadcasts, has grown into the Royal Television Society, which represents over 3,500 members from the entire spectrum of the broadcasting industry. RTS members can be found in studio services, design, management, and journalism, as well as programme making. The Society has fifteen regional centres, each running its own programme of lectures and social functions throughout the year, and these provide ideal opportunities to catch up on new ideas and technology, as well as to 'network' with people in the industry. The RTS holds conventions, symposia and workshops both in the technical and production areas.

The National Union of Journalists

Acorn House, 314–320 Grays Inn Road, London WC1X 8DP
(0171 278 7916).

With 30,000 members, the NUJ is the biggest journalists' union in the world. Members include writers, reporters, researchers, and reviewers, as well as TV and radio producers and presenters. The Union can help outsiders find training and employment in journalism and can send you a free booklet called *Careers in Journalism*. When you start work, you can apply for temporary membership where you can enjoy the benefits of free advice on rights, working conditions and rates of pay; and, if you are a freelance, an entry in the *NUJ Freelance Directory* which lists details of freelancers' work and availability. The Union will also give you a press card which is universally recognised throughout Britain. Temporary membership costs £35 for the first year, and you are asked to enclose examples of recently published work, i.e. newspaper/magazine cuttings, to substantiate that you have journalist status.

BECTU (Broadcasting, Entertainment, Cinematograph and Theatre Union)

111 Wardour Street, London W1V 4AY (0171 437 8506).

Formed from the merger of the ACTT and BETA unions, BECTU is the largest trade union in UK broadcasting. Representing both staff and freelances, it offers employment, legal and training advice. If you are going to be solely a presenter, reporter or voice-over, then BECTU will not really be relevant to you. However, if you aim to diversify into production or directing, the Union can be of benefit to you.

The Presenters' Club

123 Corporation Road, Gillingham, Kent ME7 1RG
(01634 851077).

The Presenters' Club offers members a contact file with thousands of names and addresses of people and companies like casting directors, commercial production studios and video producers who book presenters and voice-over artists. You can also buy from them the addresses on ready-printed labels, very useful for a mass mailout. You can also subscribe to weekly 'lead sheets' compiled by the club which tell you about new jobs coming up, presenter vacancies and inside information which you may not hear about just by reading the media job advertisements. This costs £65 per year. There is a telephone advice service for freelance presenters and voice-overs. There are no entry requirements and anyone is able to join the club.

Presenters' Professional Management (PPM)

PO Box 90, Sale, Cheshire M33 7PW (0161 973 0434).

Specialising in presenters' jobs and opportunities in the North, PPM organises regular radio & TV training courses for prospective broadcasters as well as mailing newsletters and leadsheets to members. The organisation also offers an appraisal service and a help line. Again, there are no entry requirements.

The Radio Academy

3–6 Langham Place, London W1A 4SZ (0171 323 3837).

The Academy has been set up for people working in the radio industry, and organises the industry's leading annual conference, the Radio Festival. They also organise seminars and conferences and publish a magazine, *The Radio Magazine*.

The Community Radio Association

15 Paternoster Row, Sheffield S1 2BX (0114 279 5219).

The CRA campaigns for the setting up and support of small radio stations which cover 'communities'. They provide advice, training and consultancy as well as organising events and conferences on community radio. They publish a journal, *Airflash*, as well as regular news sheets.

CSV Media (Community Service Volunteers)

237 Pentonville Road, St Pancras, London N1 9NJ
(0171 278 6601).

If you are an active member of a volunteer group, then CSV Media can give advice and practical help in getting your organisation's voice heard on radio and TV. They have established links with broadcasters around the UK, and through their Helpful Productions arm, produce TV and radio programmes and features of a social action nature, and organise comprehensive telephone and fact pack back-up.

FACTFILE 3

THE CONTACTS

BEFORE YOU RUSH to your word processor, some words of caution. Making a few carefully targeted applications is far better than sending photocopied CVs to everyone – 'just in case'. I have listed the main people who deal with presenters, continuity announcers and on-screen reporters, but write also to the producers or editors of TV programmes you are interested in, direct. Their names will be on the credits or in listings magazines. Remember to give anyone you contact *a reason* for being interested in you. Please check that these names still occupy the positions below; people move on fairly fast in our industry. Press officers, secretaries or switchboard operators can usually be sweet-talked into helping you out here. Good luck.

BBC NETWORK RADIO _____

BBC 1 FM, Egton House, London WIA 1AA   *(0171 765 4561/927 4575)*
Controller Radio 1   **Matthew Bannister**

BBC RADIO 2, Broadcasting House, London WIA 1AA
(0171 580 4468 / 927 4330)
Controller Radio 2   **Frances Line**

BBC RADIO 3, Broadcasting House, London WIA 1AA
(0171 580 4468 / 927 4934)
Controller Radio 3   **Nicholas Kenyon**

BBC RADIO 4, Broadcasting House, London WIA 1AA
(0171 580 4468 / 927 5337)
Controller Radio 4   **Michael Green**

BBC RADIO 5 LIVE, Broadcasting House, London WIA 1AA
(0171 580 4468 / 765 2139)
Controller Radio 5 Live   **Jenny Abramsky**

BBC World Service, PO Box 76, Bush House, The Strand, London
WC2B 4PH   *(0171 240 3456 / 257 2941)*
Director of Broadcasting   **Sam Younger**

BBC LOCAL RADIO

BBC 3 Counties Radio (Beds, Herts, Bucks), PO Box 3CR, Hastings
Street, Luton, Bedfordshire LUI 5XL   *(01582 441000)*
Programme Organiser   **Jeff Winston**

BBC Radio Berkshire, Broadcasting House, 42a Portman Road,
Reading RG3 1NB   *(01734 567056)*
Managing Editor   **Simon Major**

BBC Radio Bristol, 3 Tyndalls Park Road, Bristol BS8 1 PP
(0117 974 1 111)
Managing Editor   **Michael Hapgood**

BBC Radio Cambridgeshire, PO Box 96, 104 Hills Road, Cambridge
CB2 1LD   *(01223 259696)*
Managing Editor   **Nigel Dyson**

BBC Radio Cleveland, PO Box 95 FM, Middlesbrough, Cleveland
TS1 5DG   *(01642 225211)*
Managing Editor   **David Peel**

BBC Radio Cornwall, Phoenix Wharf, Truro TRI 1UA   *(01872 75421)*
Managing Editor   **David Farwig**

BBC Radio Cumbria, Annetwell Street, Carlisle CAI 2NA
(01228 592444)
Programme Editor   **Phil Ashworth**

BBC CWR, 25 Warwick Road, Coventry CV1 2WR   *(01203 559911)*
Programme Organiser   **Charles Hodkinson**

BBC Radio Derby, PO Box 269, Derby DE1 3HL   *(01332 361111)*
Managing Editor   **Alex Trelinski**

BBC Radio Devon, PO Box 100, St Davids Hill, Exeter EX4 4DB
(01392 215651)
Managing Editor   **Bob Button**

BBC Radio Essex, 198 New London Road, Chelmsford CM2 9XB
(01245 262393)
Managing Editor   **Margaret Hyde**

BBC Radio Foyle, 8 Northland Road, Derry, Northern Ireland BT48 7JT
(01504 262244)
Manager   **Charles Warmington**

BBC Radio Gloucestershire, London Road, Gloucester GLI 1SW
(01452 308585)
Managing Editor   **Steve Eggington**

BBC Radio GLR, 35c Marylebone High Street, London WIA 4LG
(0171 224 2424)
Managing Editor   **Steve Panton**

BBC Radio GMR, New Broadcasting House, PO BOX 951, Oxford
Road, Manchester M60 1SD   *(0161 200 2000)*
Manager   **Colin Philpott**

BBC Radio Guernsey, Commerce House, Les Banques, St Peter
Port, Guernsey, Channel Islands   *(01481 728977)*
Managing Editor   **Bob Lloyd-Smith**

BBC Radio Hereford & Worcester
In Herefordshire: 43 Broad Street, Hereford HR4 9HH   *(01432 355252)*
In Worcestershire: Hylton Road, Worcester WR2 5WW
(01905 748485)
Managing Editor   **Eve Turner**

BBC Radio Humberside, 9 Chapel Street, Hull NUI 3NU
(01482 23232)
Manager   **John Lilley**

BBC Radio Jersey, 18 Parade Road, St Helier, Jersey, Channel Islands
(01534 70000)
Station Manager   **Bob Lloyd-Smith**

BBC Radio Kent, Sun Pier, Chatham, Kent ME4 4EZ   *(01634 830505)*
Managing Editor   **To be announced**

BBC Radio Lancashire, Darwen Street, Blackburn, Lancashire BB2
2EA   *(01254 262411)*
Manager   **Steve Taylor**

BBC Radio Leeds, Broadcasting House, Woodhouse Lane, Leeds
LS2 9PN   *(0113 244 2131)*
Managing Editor **Ashley Peatfield**

BBC Radio Leicester, Epic House, Charles Street, Leicester LE1 3SH
(0116 251 3632)
Station Manager **Jeremy Robinson**

BBC Radio Lincolnshire, PO Box 219, Newport, Lincoln LN1 3XY
(01522 511411)
Managing Editor **David Wilkinson**

BBC Radio Merseyside, 55 Paradise Street, Liverpool LI 3BP
(0151 708 5500)
Manager **Richard Dukinfield**

BBC Radio Newcastle, Broadcasting Centre, Barrack Road,
Newcastle-upon-Tyne NE99 1RN   *(0191 232 4141)*
Managing Editor **Tony Fish**

BBC Radio Norfolk, Norfolk Tower, Surrey Street, Norwich NRI 3PA
(01603 617411)
Managing Editor **Tim Bishop**

BBC Radio Northampton, Compton House, Abington Street,
Northampton NN1 2BH   *(01604 239100)*
Managing Editor **Peter Davies**

BBC Radio Nottingham, York House, Mansfield Road, Nottingham
NG1 3JB   *(0115 941 5161)*
Managing Editor **Peter Hagan**

BBC Radio Oxford, 269 Banbury Road, Oxford OX2 7DW
(01865 311444)
Managing Editor **John Bright**

BBC Radio Peterborough, PO Box 957, Peterborough PE11 YT
(01733 312832)
Senior Producer **Steve Somers**

BBC Radio Sheffield, Ashdell Grove, 60 Westbourne Road, Sheffield
S10 2QU   *(0114 268 6185)*
Managing Editor **Barry Stockdale**

BBC Radio Shropshire, 2–4 Boscobel Drive, Shrewsbury SY1 3TT
(01743 248484)
Station Manager **Lawrie Bloomfield**

BBC Radio Solent, Broadcasting House, 10 Havelock Road, Southampton S01 0XR   *(01703 631311)*
Station Manager   **Chris van Schaick**

BBC Somerset Sound, 14–15 Paul Street, Taunton, Somerset TAI 3PF
(01823 252437)
Senior Producer   **Richard Austin**
(Management as for BBC Radio Bristol)

BBC Radio Stoke, Cheapside, Hanley, Stoke on Trent ST1 1JJ
(01782 208080)
Managing Editor   **John Collard**

BBC Radio Suffolk, Broadcasting House, St Matthews Street, Ipswich
Suffolk IP1 3EP   *(01473 250000)*
Managing Editor   **Ivan Howlett**

BBC Radio Sussex & Surrey, Broadcasting House, Guildford GU2 5AP
(01483 306306)
Managing Editor   **Mark Thomas**

BBC Radio Ulster, Ormeau Avenue, Belfast BT2 8HQ   *(01232 338800)*
Controller   **Robin Walsh**

BBC Wiltshire Sound, Broadcasting House, Prospect Place, Swindon,
Wiltshire SN1 3RW   *(01793 513626)*
Managing Editor   **Sandy Milne**

BBC Radio WM / WCR, PO Box 206, Pebble Mill Road, Birmingham
B5 7SD   *(0121 414 8484)*
Station Manager   **Peter Davis**

BBC Radio York, 20 Bootham Row, York Y03 7BR   *(01904 641351)*
Managing Editor   **Geoff Sargieson**

UK Commercial Radio Stations
All the following contact names are Programme Controllers or
Programme Directors, who are responsible for the hiring of on-air
presentation talent.

*NATIONAL COMMERCIAL RADIO*_____

Classic FM, 24/28 Oval Road, London NW1 7DJ   *(0171 284 3000)*
Michael Bukht

Virgin 1215, 1 Golden Square, London WIR 4DJ   *(0171 434 1215)*
Richard Skinner

Talk Radio UK, 76 Oxford Street, London W1N 0TR
(0171 636 1089)   **Jeremy Scott**

REGIONAL RADIO

Galaxy Radio (Dance music for the Severn Estuary), 25 Portland
Square, Bristol BS2 8RZ   *(0117 924 0111)*   **Tristan Bolitho**

JFM 100.4 (Jazz, soul & blues for the North West), The World Trade
Centre, Exchange Quay, Manchester M5 3EQ   *(0161 877 1004)*
Mike Henfield

Century Radio (Pop and personalities for the North East), PO Box
100, Gateshead, Tyne & Wear NE8 2YY   *(0191 477 6666)*
John Simons

Heart 100.7 FM (Soft adult music for the West Midlands), PO Box
1007, 1 The Square, 111 Broad St., Edgbaston, Birmingham BI5 1AS
(0121 626 1007)   **Paul Fairburn**

Scot FM (Adult contemporary music and speech for Central Scotland),
No. 1 Shed, Albert Quay, Leith EH6 7DN   *(0131 554 6677)*
Colin Somerville

New Regional Stations: To be advertised in 1995/6
Yorkshire, East Anglia, East Midlands, the Solent area.

LOCAL RADIO

Aire FM / Magic 828, PO Box 2000, Leeds LS3 1LR (0113 245 2299)
Jim Hicks

The Bay, PO Box 969, St Georges Quay, Lancaster LA1 3LD
(01524 848787)   **Kenni James**

Beacon Radio / WABC, 267 Tettenhall Road, Wolverhampton
WV6 0DQ   *(01902 757211)*   **Peter Wagstaff**

Boss 603, Churchill Rd, Cheltenham GL53 7EP   *(01242 255023)*
Tony Peters

Radio Borders, Tweedside Park, Galashiels, Selkirkshire TD1 3TD
(01896 59444)   **Rod Webster**

Breeze AM, Radio House, Clifftown Road, Southend-on-Sea, Essex
SS1 1SX   *(01702 430966)*   **Keith Rogers**

BRMB 96.4 FM / 1152 XTRA AM, Radio House, Aston Road North,
Birmingham B6 4BX   *(0121 359 4481)*   **Mike Owen**

Radio Broadland, 47-49 Colegate, Norwich NR3 1 DB
(01603 630621)   **Mike Stewart**

Brunel Classic Gold / GWR FM (West) PO Box 2000, Bristol
BS99 7SN   *(0117 927 9911)*   **Simon Cooper**

Bucks Broadcasting Ltd, Ringwood House, Walton Street, Aylesbury
HP21 7QP   *(01273 494253)*   **Mark Flanagan**

Buzz FM, 7 Mary Street, St Pauls, Birmingham B3 1UD
(0121 236 6777)   **Ginny Murfin**

Capital FM/Capital Gold, EustonTower, London NW1 3DR
(0171 608 6080)   **Nick Wheeler**

Central FM, Kerse Road, Stirling FK7 7YJ   *(01786 451188)*
Alec Shuttleworth

Radio Ceredigion, PO Box 600, Aberystwyth, Dyfed   *(01970 627999)*
Wynnford James

CFM, PO Box 964, Carlisle, Cumbria CAI 3NG   *(01228 818964)*
Alex Roland

Channel IO3 FM, 6 Tunnell St, St.Helier, Jersey JE2 4LU
(01534 888103)   **Richard Johnson**

Channel Travel Radio, Eurotunnel, PO Box 189, Folkestone, Kent
CT19 6YS   *(01303 272829)*   **Derek Meredith**

Chiltern Radio FM / Supergold AM, Chiltern Rd, Dunstable, Beds
LU6 1HQ   *(01582 666001)*   **Paul Chantler**

Chiltern Radio FM (East) / Supergold AM, 55 Goldington Road,
Bedford, Beds MK40 3LS   *(01234 272400)*   **Steven Marsh**

Choice FM, 16-18 Trinity Gardens, London SW9 8DP
(0171 738 7969)   **Vince Herbert**

City FM / City Gold, Stanley Street, Liverpool L69 1TQ
(0151 227 5100)   **Tony McKenzie**

Clyde 1 (FM) / Clyde 2 (AM), Clydebank, Glasgow G81 2RX
(0141 306 2200)   **Alex Dickson MBE**

CN.FM 103, Chivers Way, Histon, Cambridge CB4 4WW
(01223 235255)   **Andy Gillies**

Coast to Coast FM, Grampian TV, Queen's Cross, Aberdeen AB9 2XJ
(01224 646464)   **Martin Shannon**

Cool FM / Downtown Radio, PO Box 974, Belfast BT1 1RT
(01247 817181)   **John Rosborough**

County Sound AM, Brighton Road, Crawley, W Sussex RH11 9TT
(01293 519161)   **Martin Campbell**

Country 1035, PO Box 1035, London SW6 3QQ   (0171 384 1175)
Dan Wright

DevonAir Radio, 35–37 St David's Hill, Exeter EX4 4DA
(01392 430703)   **Dave Bowen**

eleven SEVENTY AM, PO Box 1170, High Wycombe HP13 6YT
(01494 446611)   **Andrew Phillips**

Essex Radio, Clifftown Road, Southend-on-Sea, Essex SS1 1SX
(01702 333711)   **Peter Holmes**

Fortune 1458, The Quay West Building, Trafford Wharf Road,
Manchester M17 1FL   *(0161 872 1458)*   **Steven Maskrey**

Forth FM / MAX AM, Forth House, Forth Street, Edinburgh EH1 3LF
(0131 556 9255)   **Tom Steele**

Fox FM, Brush House, Pony Road, Oxford OX4 2XR   *(01865 748787)*
Steve Ellis

Gem AM / Trent FM, 29–31 Castle Gate, Nottingham NG1 7AP
(0115 958 1731)   **Chris Hughes**

Gemini Radio, Hawthorn House, Exeter Business Park, Exeter
EX1 3QS   *(01392 444444)*   **David Rodgers**

Great North Radio, Newcastle upon Tyne NE99 1BB
(0191 496 0377)   **Jim Brown**

Great Yorkshire Gold, PO Box 777, 900 Herries Road, Sheffield
S6 1RH   *(0114 285 2121)*   **Steve Parkinson**

GWR FM (East) PO Box 2000, Swindon, Wilts SN4 7EX
(01793 853222)   **Steve Orchard**

Hallam FM, 900 Herries Road, Hillsborough, Sheffield S6 1RH
(0114 285 3333)   **Steve King**

Radio Harmony, Ringway House, Hill Street, Coventry CV1 4AN
(01203 525656)   **Suresh Joshi**

Heart FM 106.2, The Chrysalis Group, 13 Bramley Road,
London WI0 6SP   *(0171 221 2213)*   **Keith Pringle**

Heartland FM, Lower Oakfield, Pitlochry, Perthshire PH16 2DS
(01796 474040)   **Brendan Murphy**

Hereward Radio 102.7 FM, Queensgate Centre, Peterborough
PE1 1XJ   *(01733 346225)*   **Andy Gillies**

Horizon Radio, Crownhill, Milton Keynes, Bucks MK8 0AB
(01908 269111)   **Steve Power**

Invicta FM / Supergold, John Wilson Business Park, Whitstable, Kent
CT5 3QX   *(01227 772004)*   **Francis Currie**

Island FM, 12 Westerbrook, St Sampsons, Guernsey GY2 4QQ
(01481 42000)   **Kevin Stewart**

Isle of Wight Radio, 119 High Street, Newport, Isle of Wight P030 1TP
(01983 822557)   **Andy Shier**

JFM 102.2, 26/27 Castlereagh Street, London WIH 5DJ
(0171 706 4100)   **Carole Straker**

KCBC, PO Box I584, Kettering NN16 8PU   *(01536 412413)*
Robert Stiby

Kiss IOO FM, 8O Holloway Road, London N7 8JG   *(0171 700 6100)*
Gordon McNamee

Kiss 102 FM, PO Box 102, Kiss House, Portland Street, Manchester
M60 1GJ   *(0161 228 0102)*   **Mike Gray**

KL.FM 96.7, 18 Blackfriers Street, Kings Lynn, Norfolk PE30 1NN
(01553 772777)   **Stewart Francis**

Lantern Radio, 17 Market Place, Bideford, N. Devon EX39 2DR
(01237 424444)   **Fred Marden**

Leicester Sound FM, Granville House, Granville Road, Leics LE1 7RW
(0116 255 1616)   **Ron Coles**

Lincs FM, Witham Park, Waterside South, Lincoln LN5 7JN
(01522 549900)   **David Lloyd**

London Christian Radio, Suite 1D, Greencote House, Francis Street,
London SWIP IDH   *(0171 233 6705)*

London Greek Radio, Florentia Village, Vale Road, London N4 1TD
(0181 800 8001)   **T. Christodouiou**

London News Radio / London Newstalk Radio, 72 Hammersmith
Road, London W148YE   *(0171 333 0400)*   **Peter Thornton**

Radio Maldwyn, The Park, Newtown, Powys SY16 2NZ
(01686 623555)   **Mark Williams**

Marcher Coast 96.3 FM, 4l Conwy Road, Colwyn Bay, Clwyd
LL28 5AB   *(01492 534555)*   **Kevin Howard**

Marcher Gold / MFM, Mold Road, Wrexham, Clwyd L11 4AF
(01978 752202)   **Phil Roberts**

Mellow I55, 21–23 Walton Road, Frinton-on-Sea, Essex CO13 0AA
(01255 675303)   **James Hazell**

Melody Radio, 180 Brompton Road, London SW3 1HF
(0171 584 1049)   **Peter Black**

Mercia FM, Hertford Place, Coventry CV1 3TT   *(01203 633933)*
Stuart Linnell

Radio Mercury (East), Broadfield House, Brighton Road, Crawley
W. Sussex RH11 9TT   *(01293 519161)*   **Martin Campbell**

Radio Mercury (West), The Friary, Guildford, Surrey GUI 4YX
(01428 61019) **Martin Campbell**

Metro FM, Newcastle-upon-Tyne NE99 1BB
(0191 4883131) **Giles Squire**

Minster FM, PO BOX 123, Dunnington, York YO1 5ZX
(01904 488888) **Dave Lee**

Moray Firth Radio, PO Box 271, Inverness IV3 6SF   *(01463 224433)*
Thomas Prag

Nevis Radio, Inverlochy, Fort William, Inverness-shire PH33 6LU
(01379 701007) **Raymond Hervo**

96.7 BCR, Claremont Street, Lisburn Road, Belfast BT9 6JX
(01232 438500) **Mike Gaston**

North East Community Radio, Town House, Kintore, Aberdeenshire
AB51 0US *(01467 632878)* **John Dean**

Northants Radio, The Enterprise Park, Boughton Green Road,
Northampton NN2 7AH *(01604 792411)* **Colin Wilsher**

NorthSound Radio, 45 King's Gate, Aberdeen AB2 6BL
(01224 632234) **Jon R. Trowsdale**

Ocean FM, Whittle Avenue, Segensworth West, Foreham, Hants
PO15 5PA *(01489 589911)* **Jim Hicks**

Orchard FM, Haygrove House, Taunton, Somerset TA3 7BT
(01823 338448) **Phil Easton**

Piccadilly Gold / Piccadilly Key 103, 127-131 Piccadilly Plaza,
Manchester M1 4AW *(0161 236 9913)* **Mark Story/John Dash**

Pirate FM 102, Carn Brea Studios, Wilson Way, Redruth, Cornwall
TRl5 3XX *(01209 314400)* **Richard Lawley**

Plymouth Sound / Radio in Tavistock, Earl's Acre, Plymouth
PL3 4HX *(01752 227272)* **Graham Gilbert**

Power FM, Whittle Ave,Segensworth West, Fareham, Hants PO15 5PA
(01489 589911) **Jim Hicks**

The Pulse, PO Box 3000, Bradford, W. Yorks BDI 5NE
(01274 731521) **Steve Martin**

QI02.9, The Old Waterside, Duke Street, Waterside, Londonderry
(01504 46666) **Mark Wesley Lavery**

Q96, 26 Lady Lane, Paisley PAI 2LG *(0141 887 9630)* **Gerry Grant**

RadioWave, 965 Mowbray Drive, Blackpool, Lancs FY3 7JR
(01253 304965) **Simon Tate**

Ram FM, The Market Place, Derby DE1 3AA *(01332 292945)*
Dick Stone

Red Dragon FM, West Canal Wharf, Cardiff CF1 5XJ
(01222 384041) **Phil Roberts**

Red Rose Gold / Rock FM, PO Box 999, St Pauls Square, Preston
PRI 1XR *(01772 556301)* **Mark Matthews**

RTM, Tavy Bridge, Thamesmead London SE2 9UG *(0181 311 3112)*
Ken Murray

Severn Sound, Southgate Street, Gloucester GLI 2DQ
(01452 423791) **Gordon McRae**

SGR-FM (Bury), PO Box 250, Bury St Edmunds, Suffolk IP33 1AD
(01284 702622) **Mike Stewart**

SGR-FM (Ipswich), Alpha Business Park, White House Road, Ipswich,
Suffolk IP1 5LT *(01473 461000)* **Mike Stewart**

SGR Colchester, Abbeygate, 2 Whitwell Road, Colchester C02 7DF
(01206 575859) **Mike Stewart**

SIBC, Market Street, Lerwick, Shetland ZE1 OJN *(01595 5299)*
Inga Walterson

Signal Cheshire, Regent House, Heaton Lane, Stockport SK4 1BX
(0161 480 5445) **Neil Cossar**

Signal One / Signal Gold, Stoke Road, Stoke-on-Trent ST4 2SR
(01782 747047) **John Evington**

South Coast Radio / Southern FM, PO Box 2OOO, Brighton
BN41 2SS *(01273 430111)* **Chris Copsey**

South West Sound, Bankend Road, Dumfries DG1 4TH
(01387 50999) **David Lamont**

Spectrum International Radio, Endeavour House, Brent Cross,
London NW2 1JT *(0181 905 5000)* **Angela Borgnana**

Spire FM, Malthouse Lane, Salisbury, Wilts SP2 7QQ
(0172 2416644) **Chris Carnegy**

Star FM, The Observatory Shopping Centre, Slough, Berks SLI 1LH
(01753 551016) **Paul Owens**

Stray FM, PO Box 972, Station Parade, Harrogate HGI 5YF
(01423 522972) **John Wilson**

Sunrise East Midlands, Granville Rd, Leicester LE1 7RW
(01533 543002) **Raj Singh**

Sunrise FM, 30 Chapel Street, Little Germany, Bradford BDI 5DN
(01274 735043) **Usha Parmer**

Sunshine 855, Waterside, Ludlow, Shropshire SY8 1PE
(01584 873795) **Mike Melbourne**

SupaAM, 73O Pershore Road, Selly Park, Birmingham B29 7NJ
(0121 4721000) **Suresh Joshi**

Swansea Sound, Victoria Road, Gowerton, Swansea SA4 3AB
(01792 893751) **Rob Pendry**

Radio Tay, 6 North Isla Street, Dundee DD1 9UF *(01382 200800)*
Ally Ballingall

Ten 17, Latton Bush Centre, Southern Way, Harlow, Essex CM18 7BU
(01279 432415) **Peter Kerridge**

TFM Radio, Yale Crescent, Thornaby, Stockton-on-Tees TS17 6AA
(0164 2615111) **Giles Squire**

1332 The Worlds Greatest Music Station, Peterborough PE1 1XJ
(01733 346225) **Stewart Francis**

Touch AM, PO Box 99, Cardiff CF1 5YJ   *(01222 237878)*
Phil Roberts

Trent FM, 29-31 Castle Gate, Nottingham NG1 7AP   *(0115 958 1731)*
Chris Hughes

Turkish Radio, 93 Westbury Avenue, Wood Green, London N22 6SA
(0181 889 667)   **Umit Dandul**

2CR FM / Classic Gold, 5 Southcote Road, Bournemouth BH1 3LR
(01202 294881)   **Jean-Paul Hansford**

210 Classic Gold / 2 Ten FM, PO Box 2IO, Reading, Berks RG3 5RZ
(01734 413131)   **Jeff Lee**

Viking FM, Commercial Road, Hull HU1 2SG   *(01482 25141)*
Phil White

Viva 963, 26/27 Castlereagh Street, London WIH 6DJ
(0171 706 4100)   **Chris Burns**

Wear FM, Chester Road, Sunderland SR1 3SD   *(0191 515 2103)*
Karen Wheeler

Wessex FM, Trinity House, Dorchester, Dorset DT1 1DJ
(01305 250333)   **Roger Kennedy**

West Sound Radio, Holmston Road, Ayr KA7 3BE   *(01292 283662)*
Gordon McArthur

Wey Valley IO2, Prospect Place, Mill Lane, Alton, Hants GU23 2SY
(01420 544444)   **David Way**

Radio Wyvern, Barbourne Terrace, Worcester WRI 3JZ
(01905 612212)   **Sammy Southall**

Yorkshire Coast Radio, 62 Falsgrave Road, Scarborough, N. Yorks
Y012 5AX   *(01723 500962)*   **Jerry Scott**

**Proposed new services to be advertised by the Radio Authority
1995/6:**
Basingstoke, Caernarfon, Cambridge, Dundee, Fife, Great Yarmouth &
Lowestoft, Hinckley, Huddersfield, Medway Towns, North-East
Gloucestershire, Oban, Oxford, Peterhead, South-East Staffordshire,
Stratford-on-Avon, Tameside, Western Isles, Wigan, Wolverhampton,
Yorkshire Dales.

NON-UK ENGLISH-SPEAKING RADIO SERVICES _____

Blue Danube Radio, ORF Funkhaus, Argentinierstrasse 30a, 1041 Wien, Austria *(010 50 101 424)* **Tilia Herold**

Euro Jazz (Europe) Ltd, PO Box 12880 1100 AW, Amsterdam, The Netherlands *(010 31 20 420 2100)*

Irish Satellite Radio, 100 O'Connell Street, Limerick, Eire *(010 353 61 319595)* **Frank Carbury**

Long Wave Radio Atlantic 252, Summerhill Road, Trim, County Meath, Eire *(010 353 46 36655)* **Paul Kavanagh** London Office: 74 Neuman Street, London WIP 3LA *(0171 436 4012 / 0171 637 5252)* **Henry Owens**

Radio Telefis Eireann (RTE), Donnybrook, Dublin 4, Eire *(010 353 1 642350)* **Kevin Healy**

Sky Radio, Graa Wichmanian 46,1405 HB Bussum, The Netherlands London office: *0171 782 6000* **Tom Lathouwers**

UK-BASED SATELLITE AND CABLE RADIO SERVICES ____

Asda FM, Spring Bank, Astley, Manchester M29 7BR *(01942 896111)* **Jerry Rowlands**

Birmingham's BUBN, Dudley Road, Birmingham Bl8 7QH *(0121 554 5522)* **Stuart Knowles**

Bloomberg Business News, City Gate House, 39–45 Finsbury Square, London EC2 1PX *(0171 330 7500)*

Community Radio Milton Keynes (CRMK), 14 Vincent Avenue, Crownhill, Milton Keynes MK80 0AB *(01908 265266)* **Tony White**

Eclipse FM, Unit 31, Times Square Shopping Centre, High Street, Sutton, Surrey SM1 1LF *(0181 395 3388)* **Marc Damon**

Fashion FM, Top Shop, 214 Oxford Street, London WIN 9DF *(0171 927 0226)* **Peter Knott**

Network Developments (Broadcasting), PO Box 114, Windsor, Berkshire SL4 5EF *(01850 783990)* **Kieran Hughes**

Quality Europe FM / Country, PO Box 321, Camberley, Surrey GU15 2YL *(01276 676666)* **Lee Williams**

Texas Homecare FM, 29/30 Windmill Street, London WIP 1HG
(0171 580 0444) **Paul Allen**

Turkish Cable Radio, 146 Albion Road, London NI6 9PA
(0171 275 0461) **Ulus Yesilada**

United Christian Broadcasters, Cauldon Buildings, Caledonia Road,
Stoke-on-Trent ST4 2DN   *(01782 202466)* **Ann Haccius**

TV

BBC Television
BBC Television Centre, Wood Lane, London WI2 7RJ   *(0181 743 8000)*
Controller BBC 1   **Alan Yentob**
Controller BBC 2   **Michael Jackson**
Head of Children's Programmes   **Anna Home**
Head of Drama Group   **Mark Shivas**
Head of Light Entertainment   **David Liddiment**
Head of Schools Programmes   **Terence Marsh**

Kensington House, Richmond Way, London W14 OAX
(0181 895 6161)

Head of Science and Features   **David Filkin**
Head of Documentaries   **Paul Hamann**
Head of Music and Arts   **Kimberley Evans**
Head of Sports and Events Group   **Jonathan Martin**

BBC News And Current Affairs – Television
BBC Television Centre, Wood Lane, London WI2 7RJ   *(0181 743 8000)*

Editor News Programmes   **Peter Bell**
Editor Foreign Affairs   **John Simpson**
Editor Business and Economics   **Peter Jay**
Editor Social Affairs   **Polly Toynbee**

BBC World Service Television, Television Centre, Wood Lane,
London W12 7RJ   *(0181 576 2974)*
Programmes Director   **Hugh Williams**

BBC Regional Broadcasting

BBC North
New Broadcasting House, Oxford Road, Manchester M60 1SJ
(0161 200 2020)

Head of Local Programmes	**Roy Saatchi**
Head of Personnel	**Mike Fieldsend**
Youth and Entertainment Features	**Tony Moss**
Editor, Youth Programmes	**Rachel Purnell**

Broadcasting Centre, Woodhouse Lane, Leeds LS2 9PX
(0113 244 1188)

Editor News and Current Affairs	**Russell Peasgood** (*Look North*)
Assistant Editors	**David Lewis, Jon Williams**

Broadcasting Centre, Barrack Road, Newcastle upon Tyne NE99 2NE
(0191 232 1313)

Editor News	**Ian Cameron** (*Look North*)
Assistant Editors	**Iain Williams, Richard Porter**

BBC Midlands & East
Broadcasting Centre, Pebble Mill Road, Birmingham B5 7QQ
(0121 414 8888)

Head of News & Current Affairs	**Rick Thompson** (*Midlands Today*)
Head of Personnel	**Kevin Hosier**
Head of TV Drama	**Barry Hanson**
Managing Editor Network TV Leisure Programmes	**John King**
Manager Planning & Programme Services	**Jenny Brewer**

East Midlands Broadcasting Centre, York House, Mansfield Road,
Nottingham NG1 3JB   *(0115 947 2395)*

News Editor East Midlands   **Roger Protheroe** (*East Midlands Today*)

St Catherine's Close, All Saints Green, Norwich, Norfolk NRI 3ND
(01603 619331)

News Editor East	**Graham Henshaw** (*Look East*)
Manager Personnel & Administration	**Pat Hewison**

BBC South
Broadcasting House, Whiteladies Road, Bristol BS8 2LR (0117 973 2211)

Head of Television Features	**Peter Salmon**
Head of Local Programmes West	**John Conway**
Personnel Officer Local Programmes	**Annette Clements**

Broadcasting House, Havelock Road, Southampton S01 OXQ
(01703 226201)

Editor News and Current Affairs	**Andy Griffee** (*South Today*)
Manager Personnel	**Caroline Prendergast**

Broadcasting House, Seymour Road, Mannamead, Plymouth PL3 5BD
(01752 229201)

Editor News & Current Affairs	**Tony Maddox** (*Spotlight*)
Manager Personnel	**Jane Mair**
BBC South East	

Elstree Centre, Clarendon Road, Borehamwood, Hertfordshire WD6 1JF
(0181 953 6100)

Editor Newsroom South East	**Guy Pelham**
Editor First Sight	**Alison Rooper**
Manager Personnel	**Maureen Wicker**

BBC Wales
Broadcasting House, Llandaff, Cardiff CF5 2YQ   (01222 572888)

Head of News & Current Affairs	**Aled Eirug** (*Wales Today*)
Head of Music & The Arts, Wales	**Hilary Boulding**
Head of Factual Programmes	**Roy Davies**
Editor, Radio Wales	**Gaynor Vaughan-Jones**

BBC Scotland
Broadcasting House, Queen Margaret Drive, Glasgow G12 8DG
(0141 330 2345)

Head of Television Scotland	**Colin Cameron** (*Reporting Scotland*)
Head of News	**Kenneth Cargill**
Head of Music & Arts	**John Archer**
Head of Comedy	**Colin Gilbert**

BBC Northern Ireland
Broadcasting House, Ormeau Avenue, Belfast BT2 8HQ
(01232 338000)

Head of Programmes	**Patrick Loughrey**
Head of Personnel	**Ruth Laird**
Editor News	**Tom Kelly** (*Inside Ulster*)
Chief Producer, Features	**Colin Lewis**
Chief Producer, Sport	**Jim Neilly**
Chief Producer, Music and Arts	**Ian Kirk-Smith**

COMMERCIAL TELEVISION (Terrestrial)

Anglia Television, Anglia House, Norwich NR1 3JG   *(0160 361 5151)*
Director of News: **Jim Wilson** (*Anglia News; East & West*)
Head of Presentation: **Granville Jenkins**

Anglia News centres:
Cambridge: 01223 467076   Chelmsford: 01245 357676
Ipswich: 01473 226157   Luton: 01582 29666
Milton Keynes: 01908 691660   Northampton: 01604 24343
Peterborough: 01733 346677

Border Television, Television Centre, Carlisle CAI 3NT   *(01228 25101)*
News Editor: **Neil Robinson** (*Lookaround*)
Head of Presentation: **Eric Hadwin**

Carlton Television, 101 St Martin's Lane, London WC2N 4AZ
(0171 240 4000)
Editor, Factual Programmes: **Marion Bowman**
Head of Presentation: **Wendy Chapman**
(Carlton's *London Tonight* is made by London News Network,
0171 827 7700)

Central Independent Television, Central House, Birmingham BI 2JP
(0121 643 9898)

Controller, Regional Programmes:	**Steve Clark**
Controller, News:	**Laurie Upshon** (*Central News*)
Head of Presentation:	**David Jamieson**

Central TV studios:
Nottingham: 0115 986 3322   Oxford: 01235 554123

Channel Television, The TV Centre, La Pouquelaye, St Helier, Jersey
JE2 3ZD   *(01534 68999)*
Director of Operations: **Roy Manning**

Channel 4 Television, 124 Horseferry Road, London SWIP 2TX
(0171 396 4444)
Personnel: **Gill Monk**
Director of Programmes: **John Willis**
Head of Presentation: **Cherry Cole**

Channel 4 Breakfast Franchise: *The Big Breakfast,* Planet 24, 195
Marsh Wall, London El4 9SG   *(0171 712 9300)*
Editor: **Charlie Parsons**

GMTV, The London Television Centre, Upper Ground, London
SE1 9LT   *(0171 827 7000)*
Director of Programmes: **Peter McHugh**
Editor: **Liam Hamilton**

Grampian Television, Queens Cross, Aberdeen AB9 2XJ
(01224 646464)
Head of News: **Alistair Gracie** *(North Tonight)*
Head of Features: **Ted Brocklebank**

Granada Television, Quay Street, Manchester M60 9EA
(0161 832 7211)
Editor, *Granada Tonight:*   **Susan Woodward**
Head of Regional Programmes: **Michael Spencer**

Granada studios & offices:
Liverpool: 0151 709 9393   Lancaster: 01524 60688
Chester: 01244 313966   Blackburn: 01254 690099

HTV Wales, Culverhouse Cross, Cardiff CF5 6XJ   *(01222 590590)*
Controller of Programmes: **Don Hill-Davies**
Head of News: **Elis Owen** *(Wales at Six)*

HTV West, Bath Road, Bristol BS4 3HG   (00117 977 8366)
Director of Programmes: **Steve Matthews**
Head of News: **Ken Rees** *(HTV News)*

London Weekend Television, The London Television Centre, Upper
Ground, London SE1 9LT   *(0171 620 1620)*
Entertainment Controller: **John Kaye-Cooper**
Producer, The London Programme: **Jim Allen**

Meridian Broadcasting, Television Centre, Southampton S02 OTA
(01703 222555)
Controller of Regional Programmes: **Mary McAnally**
Controller of News: **Jim Raven** *(Meridian Tonight)*

RTE, Radio Telefis Eirann, Donnybrook, Dublin 4, Eire.
(010 353 1 643111)

Scottish Television, Cowcaddens, Glasgow G2 3PR   *(0141 332 9999)*
Head of Programmes: **David Scott**
Producer, Factual Programmes: **Paul Murricane** *(Scotland Today)*

S4C, Sianel Pedwar Cymru, Parc ty Glas, Llanishen, Cardiff CF4 5DV
(01222 747444)
Director of Programmes: **Deryck Williams**
Head of Personnel: **Ifan Roberts**

Tyne Tees Television, Television Centre, Newcastle upon Tyne,
NE1 2AL   *(0191 261 0181)*
Controller of Regional Programmes & Producer, *Tyne Tees Today:*
Olwyn Hocking

Ulster Television (UTV), Havelock House, Ormeau Road, Belfast
BT71EB   *(01232 328122)*
Head of Factual Programmes: **Michael Beattie**
Producer, *UTV Live at Six:*   **Rob Morrison**

Westcountry Television, Western Wood Way, Language Science
Park, Plymouth, Devon PL7 5BG   *(01752 333333)*
Controller of News: **Richard Myers** *(Westcountry Live)*
Controller of Features: **Jane Clarke**
Head of Presentation: **Steve Ellis**

Yorkshire Television, The Television Centre, Kirkstall Road, Leeds
LS3 1JS   *(0113 243 8283)*
Director of Programmes: **Grant McKee**
Producer, Calendar   **Ali Rashid**
Head of Presentation: **Robert Bairstow**

SATELLITE AND CABLE TV

The Children's Channel, 9–13 Grape Street, London WC2H 8DR
(0171 240 3422) **Andy Shaw**

CNN International, CNN House, 19–22 Rathbone Place, London
WIP 1DF *(0171 637 6700)* **Eason Jordan**

Country Music Television (Europe), UA Programming, 16 Bonny
Street, London NW1 9PG *(0171 813 5000)* **Joyce Taylor**

Eurosport, 15 Berner Street, London WIP 3DE *(0171 580 4342)*

MTV Europe, Hawley Crescent, London NW1 8TT *0171 284 7777*
Director of Talent: **Harriet Brand**
Director, Programming and Production: **Brent Hansen**

Open Campus TV, Blackburn College, Fielden Street, Blackburn,
Lancs BB2 1LH *(01254 55144)* **Len Adam**

B SKY B, 6 Centaurs Business Park, Grant Way, Isleworth, Middlesex
TW7 5QD *(0171 705 3000)*
Production Manager: **John Rowe**
Head of News and Sport: **Ian Frykberg**

Superchannel, Melrose House, 14 Lanark Square, London EI4 9QD
(0171 418 9418)
Head of Programming: **Suzette Knittl**
Press Officer: **Sarah Holmes**

Wire TV, c/o United Artists Programming, Twyman House, 16 Bonny
Street, London NW1 9PG *(0171 813 5000)*
Head of Programmes: **Nigel Haunch**

NEWS CONTACTS

ABC News Intercontinental, 8 Carburton Street, London WIP 7DT
(0171 637 9222)

CBS News (UK), 68 Knightsbridge, London SWIX 7LL
(0171 581 4801)

CNN International, CNN House, 19–22 Rathbone Place, London
WIP 1DF *(0171 637 6700/6800)*

Independent Radio News, 1 Euston Centre, London NW1 3JG
(0171 388 4558) **John Perkins**

ITN Radio News, 200 Grays Inn Road, London WC1X 8XZ
(0171 430 4814) **Dervil Fitzsimons**

ITN, 200 Grays Inn Road, London WC1X 8XZ *(0171 833 3000)*
Stewart Purvis

The London News Network, The London Television Centre, Upper
Ground, London SE1 9LT *(0171 827 7700)*

Network News, Crownhill, Milton Keynes MK8 OAB *(01908 269111)*
Angus Moorat

Reuters Television, 200 Grays Inn Road, London WC1X 8XZ
(0171 250 1122) **Mark Wood**

Sky News, 6 Centaurs Business Park, Grant Way, Isleworth, Middlesex
TW7 5QD *(0171 705 3000)* **John O'Loan**

WTN, Worldwide Television News, The Interchange, Oval Road,
Camden Lock, London NW1 *(0171 410 5200)*

ORGANISATIONS AND OTHER CONTACTS

AA Roadwatch, 0181 954 7344

Association of Independent Radio Companies 0171 727 2646

Association for Media Education in England 01924 830261

BBC Recruitment Services 0181 752 5252

British Film Institute 0171 255 1444

**Broadcasting Entertainment Cinematograph and Theatre Union
(BECTU)** 0171 278 3686

Broadcast Magazine 01732 770823 (Subs)
0171 837 9263 (Editorial)

Broadcast Production Guide 0171 837 1212

Cable Television Association 0171 222 2900   0800 300750

Commonwealth Broadcasting Association   0181 752 5252 ext. 25022

Community Radio Association   0114 279 5219

CSV Media   0171 278 6601

Edinburgh International Television Festival   0171 379 4519

Equity   0171 379 6000

European Television Directory   01491 574671

Film and Television Freelance Training ("FT2")   0171 734 5141

Hospital Broadcasters' Association   0171 402 8815   01245 451114

International Weather Productions   0171 284 3485

ITV Network Centre   0171 843 8000

Meteorological Office   01344 420 242

National Council for the Training of Journalists   01279 430009

National Council for the Training of Broadcast Journalists
0181 940 0694

National Film and Television School   01494 671234

National Union of Journalists (NUJ)   0171 278 7916

Networking (Broadcasting Contacts for Women)   0113 242 8646

Periodicals Training Council   0171 836 8798

RAC Road Data   0181 681 1928

Radio Academy   0171 323 3837

Radio Authority   0171 430 2724

Royal Television Society   0171 430 1000

Scottish Broadcast and Film Training   0141 332 2201

Skillset (Industry Training Organisation)   0171 306 8585

Society of Women Writers and Journalists   0181 529 0886

Women's Audio Visual Education Scheme   0171 430 1076

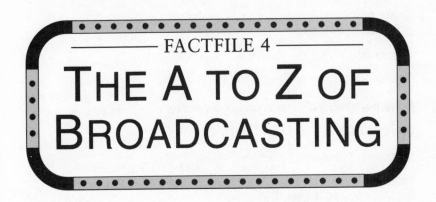

THE A TO Z OF BROADCASTING

HERE ARE SOME OF those curious broadcasting terms and expressions you're likely to come across. This A to Z is by no means all-inclusive, but it will give you a good grounding in the broadcasting terms in use today, and may help you to decipher scripts.

You'll notice the abundance of television terms compared to the relatively small selection from radio. Is this because TV is crammed full of esoteric jargon, or is it because in radio they simply speak English?

Italics are used to show that a term is given its own entry in this glossary.

Access Television
Programmes made by organisations or individuals outside professional TV companies, usually to put their own points of view across. Also called 'Community Television'.

'Action!'
Given by the director when camera and sound are running up to the correct speed. This is a cue for the performer(s) to start.

Actuality
The 'actual' unscripted sound recorded in a location, as against sound effects or narration added back in the studio.

Ad-lib
Improvised, unscripted speech.

ADO
Ampex Digital Optics. A brand name of a video effects machine. The umbrella term for all these gadgets is *DVE* or Digital Video Effects.

AFM

Assistant Floor Manager. Provides back-up and assistance to the *Floor Manager.*

AI

Appreciation index. The AI is a form of qualitative research which ascertains the 'enjoyment value' of a transmitted television programme. A show may have low viewing figures, but a high AI.

AM

Amplitude Modulation. The system of radio broadcasting used on long, medium and short wave. The amplitude of the carrier wave is modulated by the broadcast signal. This system is prone to interference, unlike *FM* or Frequency Modulation.

Ammy drammy

Slang, derisory term arts producers have for amateur dramatic shows.

Analogue recording

Where the recorded sound or vision is stored by a continuously changeable magnetic flux on moving tape. (As against *digital recording* where a computerised numerical system is used.)

Answerprint

A colour print of the finished, edited, negative film used as a viewing copy, before the better quality SHOWPRINT is made for transmission.

ARBITRON

American radio's main audience research system.

Arriflex

Trade name of German-made film camera.

Artfile

Brand name of one of a range of graphics machines which can create logos, maps, etc, and can colour in monochrome pictures. Other names you may encounter: Paintbox, HAL, Harriet, Harry.

Assemble editing

Recording chunks of video pictures and sound onto completely blank tape, unlike *insert editing* where pictures and/or sound are recorded onto a video tape which has pre-recorded *control track*, which gives greater flexibility. Assemble editing is usually only used when making compilations of already-edited programmes.

Assistant cameraman
This person is responsible for loading film magazines, checking equipment and putting on *clapperboards.* You rarely have assistants with video camera operators unless the production is complex.

Aston
Brand name of a TV caption generator, used on-air in the *gallery,* or in the post-production suite.

Autocue
Brand name for a system where the presenter reads the scripts from a TV monitor which is reflected over the camera lens to give the impression that the words have been memorised. Another brand is Portaprompt.

Available light
Light from the sky, windows or existing interior illumination; as opposed to putting up TV lights on location.

BA
Broadcasting Assistant. A semi-technical, semi-production job in a radio station. May also be called Technical Assistant, or Studio Manager.

Baby legs
A mini camera tripod used to obtain steady, low shots.

Back announcement
A reference to a song, item or programme just broadcast.

Backing track
A pre-recorded audio tape, used to perform over. For example, a TV music show is much easier to produce with a ready-recorded instrumental track for artists to sing along to.

Barndoors
The black metal hinged doors around a light, used to control the direction of the light.

Barney
A padded cover on a film or video camera used to muffle motor noise in quiet filming situations.

Best boy
General 'gofer' on a large studio stage (usually film/drama). Responsible for getting and shifting lights, props, equipment, or all three.

BETACAM SP

Sony's camcorder system, widely in use in the professional TV world. It uses metal tape in cassettes. The system is incompatible with the now obsolete domestic BETACORD video cassette system.

BITC

(Pronounced Bit-Cee.) Stands for Burnt-in Time Code. The *timecode* is displayed in a small *letterbox* on screen, so you can tell exactly where you are on a videotape. This information is encoded on the tape but is never broadcast.

Blacked tape

Video tape with *control track* recorded on it, so *insert editing* can be performed. Viewing it will show a completely black screen, unlike virgin blank tape, which will show 'snow' or 'hash'.

Blocking

Rehearsal of a scene where camera and performers' movements are sorted out, before filming starts.

Blonde

A large (2kW) light used in TV studios and on location. It has a yellow-coloured head, hence 'blonde'.

Boom

A long or telescopic pole from which a microphone is suspended. 'Boom shadow' is where this pole ruins the shot by causing shadows.

Booth

A soundproofed room where voice-overs work. There is usually a talkback system installed to achieve two-way communication with the control room.

BPM

Beats per minute. A guide to the speed (tempo) of a recorded song.

Bracketing

A camera operator may ask for a retake on a scene to ensure the exposure is correct. He may take three versions, a fraction of a stop (an f-stop) apart (darker to brighter) to make sure a good one is 'in the can'.

Breakthrough

Unwanted sound 'breaking' into a soundtrack or audio channel. This can happen if many radio microphones are being used on one location.

Bulk eraser
Machine for wiping magnetic audio or video tape, which simply consists of a magnetic coil. Remember to switch off after use unless you want a buzzing, molten fire hazard. You may encounter a huge industrial version with a steel semi-circular lid, affectionately known as a 'fishfryer'.

Burn out
Where over-exposure renders white or light parts of a picture devoid of detail.

Buzzer cue
A communication method between a TV control room (*gallery*) and *VT* or *Telecine* operators. For example, the Director may say on the *talkback*, 'Cued on item 5, VT 3?' The appropriate operator in the depths of the VT area responds one buzz for 'yes', and two buzzes for 'no'. The thinking behind this system is that VT people are too busy pushing buttons and lacing up tapes to engage their inbuilt, organic, vocal system.

Buzz track
Background atmosphere recording which is used to even out any sound mismatches in edited film or video. Sometimes called '*wildtrack*'.

BVU
Broadcast Video U-matic. A Sony video system that uses inch tape in cassettes. More bulky than the *BETACAM* cassette system, the pictures and sound quality are not as good either. Becoming obsolete.

Cable basher
Junior film crew member whose unenviable job it is to put out and wind up camera, audio and lighting cables in all situations and weathers.

Call sheet
Details of locations and times for presenters, actors and contributors. Sometimes combined with *shooting schedules.*

Camcorder
A camera and recorder in one unit.

Camera script
A list of shot details for use by the camera operator.

Cans
Slang for headphones. Not to be confused with 'in the can', which means completed (recording, processing, editing, whatever).

Caption card
Simply a piece of cardboard used for mounting artwork or rub down letters. It is placed on a caption stand, and a studio camera focuses on it.

Caption generator
A machine which can create words for titles and credits which can be superimposed over pictures.

CAR
Central Apparatus Room. This has switching and amplification gear in, along with racks of equipment which are controlled from the *gallery*.

Cart machine
An audio player/recorder using loops of tape in cartridges. 'Carts' (cartridges) are usually in 20-, 40-, 70-, 90- and 100-second lengths for radio jingles, commercials and *promos.* There are also 3.5- or 5.5-minute carts to record music tracks. The system is gradually being replaced by instant access digital storage systems.

Catchline
The 'title' of a news story or item printed at the top of the script. If the story has been originated from a freelance reporter, it is important to keep the exact title when retyping as payments are made on catchlines.

Charisma
A particular type of video effects generator.

Cherry picker
A form of hydraulic platform used for high camera shots. You may also encounter a Simon hoist.

Chinagraph
Wax pencil, usually yellow or white, used to write on or mark tape or film.

Chromakey
See *CSO.*

Chrominance signal
See *Luminance signal.*

Chyron
Trade name of a type of TV caption generator.

Clapperboard
A board with 'scene' and 'take' information. This is written on by hand

and is used in editing to synchronise the film pictures and the sound-track. Not needed for video.

Clashcode

A code assigned to TV or radio commercials in the 'traffic' department (nothing to do with road traffic) so that the computer responsible for spot rotation will not place two clients with similar products next to each other in the transmitted commercial break. There can be clashcodes for voice-over and style as well.

Clean feed

The studio output sent to another location, say, *OB* point, but without the contribution from that location. This prevents *feedback* or howl-round.

Clip

A short extract of film or videotape.

Clock

A countdown clock before a TV programme, which includes identification and technical information. The picture cuts to black at three seconds to zero, in case the clock is accidentally selected to air. The staff in the *gallery* watch the clocks on their monitors.

Coldfade

A description of how a record ends. The song has a definite ending but it is not as sudden as one that is described as having an 'end'. Usually it sounds bad to talk over a cold fade.

Colour balance

Achieved by 'lining up' an electronic camera to accept a white card shown to the lens as true white, even in non-daylight. The camera will then show natural colours.

Colour bars

A 'rainbow' effect test signal used in TV engineering.

COMMAG

Sound and vision on one strip of film with sound on magnetic stripe. When sound is on a separate spool, it is called *sepmag*, and is more flexible to edit.

Commentary

The voice-over which is usually recorded on the final *dub* of the film. Also called voice-over (*VO*) or written as OOV (out of vision).

COMOPT
Film with optical soundtrack down the side. It is a wiggly line through which light is shone; a sensor the other side turns the light into sound.

Compressor
A device which electronically reduces the dynamic range of an audio signal. Can make the signal sound 'punchier' or 'louder'.

Continuity
(1) The department of studios where TV programmes and other elements are arranged into a 'continuous' station output. (See *Presentation*.) Sometimes videotapes are played in at the TV station, sometimes the 'network feed' is taken, which is common to all BBC or ITV stations.
(2) A detailed record taken while filming, so shots taken in non-continuous shooting can be edited together correctly. Notes are taken about costume, hair, make-up, position of actors, presenters, etc. Polaroid cameras are widely used on location to assist with continuity.

Control track
Invisible electronic coding recorded onto video tape, a kind of 'electronic sprocket hole' which ensures stable, clear pictures. A tape with control track can be used for *insert editing*, where pictures and/or sound can be replaced without affecting the rest of the edited videotape.

Crossing the line
Confusing viewers' perspective and sense of direction of successive shots by changing position of camera by 180 degrees during filming.

CSO
Chromatic Separation Overlay, also known as Chromakey. When shooting a scene against a chosen colour, an electronic device can fill all the coloured areas with pictures from another source. Used extensively in weather bulletins. Cobalt blue is normally chosen because it is a colour far away from flesh tones.

Cue burn
This is damage to a vinyl disc caused by continuous cueing up at the start.

Cue dot
Electronic square at corner of screen, used to cue programmes and commercial breaks in continuity suites. In British television, five seconds after the cue dot disappears, something else should appear.

Cutaway
A shot usually showing a detail of what is being talked about on the

screen, for example, during a recorded interview. Cutaways hide *jump-cuts* in the edited master shot.

Cyclorama
The large neutral backing of a set, usually made of stretched fabric. It provides a more attractive background than the studio wall.

DAT
Digital Audio Tape. Very small cassettes which record premium quality digital sound.

Depth of field
The part of a shot which is in focus.

Digital recording
Sound or pictures encoded and stored using a computerised numerical system as opposed to the old *analogue* system of recording continuously variable flux on a moving tape. With digital recording, the tape can be copied or dubbed with no loss of quality.

Director
This person is responsible for all the creative decisions that make the finished television programme.

Dissolve
To create a sound or vision transition where one sound/picture fades and the next appears. Same as 'mix'.

Dolby
A patented system which reduces the hiss on the audio tracks. There are these non-compatible types: A + SR for professional use; B for domestic; and C for semi-professional use. There is another, less often used system called 'dbx'.

Dolly
A trolley used to move camera around smoothly. Can also be used as a verb.

Domestic cut-off
The outer frame of a domestic television picture, lost when seen at home on a domestic set. As in 'Don't worry about the stain on your tie, it will be in domestic cut-off!'

Double header
The presentation of a programme by two people.

Down-the-line interview

Where people in different locations conduct an interview looking at each other on television monitors or listening on radio headphones.

Dropout

A slight loss of picture or sound due to particles of magnetic oxide being rubbed off tape after prolonged use. Be aware of this when reusing video or audio tape.

Dry hire

The hiring of equipment like cameras, microphones and autocue gear without operators. With 'wet hire' you get humans included in the package.

DSK

Down Stream Keyer. Usually a paddle on a *gallery* desk by which captions can be faded in or out over the studio output.

DTS

Daily Transmission Schedule. A BBC Television term to describe the details of the times that the regions have to 'opt out' and 'opt in' from network programmes from London.

Dub

To transfer recorded sound or vision to another tape adding extra tracks, or processing it in some way. Can also mean rerecording soundtracks into another language.

DVE

Digital Video Effect. A machine which can distort, tumble, twist, spin or squeeze pictures.

Edge numbers

Numbers printed onto the edge of film stock by the manufacturers to aid identification. Also known as 'key numbers'.

Editor

(1) The creative technical person who cuts film or edits video tape.
(2) The boss of a programme series or news operation, responsible for the total content.

Emergency cue tag

Used on live television programmes. A sentence-worth of extra introduction to a *VT* insert, written by the presenter. Used if VT is run late for whatever reason; the presenter then has valuable seconds of sensible extra introduction without an embarrassing gap or fluffed ad-lib.

Emergency tape

DAT cassette or reel-to-reel audio tape on ten-inch-diameter reels, kept in radio on-air studios to cover fire evacuations or other emergencies. An 'obit tape' of soft music is also kept here from transmission on the news of the death of a member of the royal family.

End board

A *clapperboard* put at the end of a take rather than at the beginning. It is always shot upside down.

Ends

Where a record has a distinct ending; you can't talk over it like you can a song which 'fades'.

ENG Crew

Electronic News Gathering. An ITV term to describe a lightweight video camera crew as opposed to a crew that uses film. The BBC sometimes calls this system PSC or Portable Single Camera.

EQ

Equalisation of sound. Boosting or cutting bass and treble.

Establisher shot

A general view (*GV*) of a location so that viewers can get their bearings.

Extra

An actor who appears on screen but doesn't say anything and is not individually directed. A *walk-on* is given some form of direction, and some may have a token speaking part. Also known as 'supporting artists'.

Eyeline

The direction in which the presenter or artist is looking.

Fade

A song which slowly reduces in volume at the end.

FDU

Fade down and up. A TV continuity term meaning that programme sound and vision is faded down and another source is faded up.

Feedback

A piercing sound caused when a microphone picks up its own amplified output from nearby loudspeakers or headphones, also known as 'howl-round'.

Fire lane
Lines on TV studio floors mark this space which cannot be blocked by cameras, other equipment or people. The *Floor Manager* or Assistant Floor Manager (*AFM*) police this.

Fish eye lens
An extremely wide-angle lens.

Flat
A flat piece of scenery in a TV set.

Floor Manager
This person, in direct radio contact with staff in the *gallery*, is responsible for assisting and co-ordinating all the other staff on the studio floor. This can range from distributing scripts to camera operators and presenters to ensuring that *fire lanes* are kept clear of props and furniture. They can also provide visual signals to presenters to tell them when to speak or wind up, to reinforce the director's audio commands.

FM
Frequency Modulation. The system of stereo radio broadcasting used on the VHF waveband 88–108 MHz. The carrier frequency is modulated by the broadcast signal. FM is less susceptible to crackles and interference than *AM* or Amplitude Modulation.

Foldback
A sound signal sent to a loudspeaker in the studio as a cueing or monitoring device for the presenter or performer.

Footage
The length of film in feet.

Frame
A single picture stored on video tape or in a length of film. In UK television there are 25 frames per second on video tape.

Freeze frame
One film frame, or single video picture, 'frozen' on screen.

Gaffer
The main electrician or lighting person on location or in a studio. His assistant is called a *Best Boy* on film sets.

Gaffer tape
Thick, wide tape generally used to stick down cables in safety on a studio floor.

Gain
An increase in level of audio or video signal.

Gallery
The soundproofed control room for a TV studio where all sound and vision is controlled. Gallery personnel consist of director, PA, vision mixer, prompting device operator, and others.

Gel (Slang: Jelly)
A filter placed over a light. It is usually coloured and creates mood or matches daylight.

Generation
Dub a master video tape onto another reel or cassette and it becomes a second generation copy. The quality becomes progressively worse as further copies are made unless you are working with *digital recordings.*

Goldfishing
Where someone on screen is seen to be mouthing something, but can't be heard.

Grams
Machines which play vinyl records.

Green room
The area reserved for guests of and contributors to a television programme where they wait before being ushered to the studio floor by floor staff. Also known as the Hospitality room (or in cynical television stations as the 'Hostility room').

Grips
People on a film crew who transport and operate equipment such as camera dollies.

G spool
One-inch video tape on small plastic spools. Most TV commercials, pop videos and film clips are sent out on these spools.

GTS
Greenwich Time Signal.

Gun mike
Microphone which picks up sound from only one distinct direction.

GV
General view or *establisher shot*.

Hal, Harry, Harriet
Brand names of digital graphics and animation systems.

Handbasher
Portable battery-operated light often used for news filming.

Headroom
Amount of space above a person's head in frame.

Heads
Components of an audio or video recorder which erase, record or play-back. They're delicate and must be clean for best results.

Highband
A *BVU* video cassette system which is of broadcast quality. The 'Low Band' system uses similar cassettes, but is electronically incompatible with 'High Band' and gives inferior quality.

Hook up
A daily conference between the BBC TV presentation department in London and the regions to decide on the duration and timing of *opt-outs*. Everybody can speak to and hear everybody else.

Ikegami
Brand name of a Japanese camera manufacturer, usually shortened to 'Ikki' as in 'Can you put my Ikki on the tripod?' You'll find that actual machines are often referred to by their name of manufacture in broadcasting.

Inject
A live contribution usually from a region into a network programme. This is distinct from 'opting out' where the region ignores the network feed and puts out its own programme.

Insert editing
Where you edit onto a video tape which has a prerecorded *control track*. This is more flexible than *assembly editing* because you can erase or add just vision and/or sound to your finished tape.

Jackfield
Rows of electric sockets which can connect up different equipment inputs and outputs. Also known as 'patchbay'.

Jumpcut
A cut which doesn't follow the continuity of action. For example, a TV interviewee's reply may have a chunk cut out of the middle; this must be covered by a *cutaway* to avoid a jarring jumpcut.

Keylight
The main light source falling onto a set or person.

Lacing
Threading audio tape, film or video round heads and rollers of a machine.

Lastolite
A trade name for a circular hoop of wire across which is stretched an area of reflective material. Useful on locations to even out shadows on faces in bright sunlight.

Leader
A length of plastic tape spliced onto the front of an audio tape or film to allow easy *lacing* and which cannot be recorded onto. It also gives time for the machine to run up to speed before the recording starts.

Leevers-Rich
Trade name for a make of reel-to-reel tape recorder. Other makes of reel-to-reel or quarter-inch audio machines you may encounter: Studer, Revox, Ampex, Ferrograph, Otari.

Legal ID
A radio station's actual registered name like 'North Weshington Community Radio' rather than the main slogan name heard on-air, for example, 'Power 99'.

Letterbox
(1) A black or semi-transparent strip usually at the bottom of the screen which carries subtitles or, in the case of *off-line* video *dubs*, carries *timecode* numbers.
(2) Where a widescreen film is shown in its correct picture format, leaving black above and below the picture on a TV screen.

Library music
Special discs of 'non-*needletime*' music and effects not for sale to the

public, and not under the control of Phonographic Performance Limited (PPL). Under licence from the MCPS (Mechanical Copyright Protection Society), this music is used for commercials and backing music. Sometimes called 'mood' music.

Lighting cameraperson
A person responsible for setting up lights on location as well as operating the camera.

Line up
Setting up of equipment which in TV should take place before every studio or edit session. This is done to ensure that the electronic circuitry is working at its best.

Lip microphone
A microphone which has to be held very close to the presenter's mouth. Used in very noisy surroundings such as football matches.

Location
Any place used for filming, outside a studio.

Looking room
Giving one person in frame more room in the direction he's looking in, than behind him.

Lot
A place where exterior sets are built.

LS
Long shot.

LSC
Lead, Sound and Cut. A method where the sound from the next scene is heard before the pictures are seen. This takes the attention away from the edit and makes the transition less jarring. Used for dramatic effect as well as in TV continuity.

Luminance signal
The black and white part of the video signal. The *chrominance signal* provides the colour information.

Magazine
A metal casing which contains film. This clips on to the film camera. Magazines have to be loaded in a light-proof changing bag, usually by the assistant cameraman.

M & E track
Soundtrack with music and effects.

Marantz
Trade name for a compact, portable cassette-recorder which uses normal domestic cassettes, although professionals should use quality chrome or metal cassettes with *Dolby* selected. The recording from the cassette has to be transferred or dubbed onto quarter-inch tape, or onto a digital system like Audiofile, before you can edit.

Master shot
A wide shot taken of the whole of a song in a pop video or a scene in a drama in case a close-up or *cutaway* doesn't work out.

Master tape
Edited final programme, pre-recorded and ready for transmission.

MCR
(Radio:) Master Control Room, back in the studio.
(Television:) Mobile Control Room or *scanner*, out on location.

MCU
Medium Close-Up. Standard waist-upwards framing of subject. Also known as 'Mid Shot'.

Mixer
A machine which can fade up and down and mix together the outputs of sound or video channels.

Monitor
Broadcast-quality screen which takes a video input, and cannot receive off-air sound or vision. Used in a *gallery* on the studio floor, or out on location.

Multiburst
A black and white test pattern, usually generated by *VT* machines.

Mute shot
Filmed without sound.

Needletime
Describes a commercial record release registered under PPL (Phonographic Performance Ltd) which radio and TV stations have to pay for in order to broadcast. Most stations have a PPL 'blanket licence'

to use needletime records in general programming, but special permission must be granted to use the music in advertising.

Newsgate
A predetermined time before a news bulletin after which a breaking story will not make it to air. This is to stop a non-substantiated story becoming broadcast or from being presented in a hurried, unprofessional fashion. The time is usually five minutes for radio bulletins, ten minutes for television. It is always being broken by eager news editors who want an exclusive!

Newslink
Radio commercials placed next to news bulletins at a premium advertising rate.

Nicam
(Near Instantaneous Companded Audio Modulation.) The system used to broadcast quality stereo sound from terrestrial television transmitters in the UK.

Noddy
A *cutaway* shot of reporter 'nodding' at the interviewee, used to cover a *jumpcut.*

Noise
Poor *signal-to-noise ratio* when recording. This can give rise to 'hiss' on audio tapes and 'snow' on video signals.

OB
Outside Broadcast. A live TV or radio programme which is originated outside a studio.

Off line
A rough video edit on cheaper equipment to check the look and duration of a feature or programme before using the broadcast-standard On Line suite. Usually done on VHS or U-Matic cassettes with *timecode* burnt into a *letterbox* on each frame. (See *BITC*.)

Omnidirectional microphone
Picks up sound from all directions.

Open talkback
Where studio personnel can hear what is going on, in the *gallery* all the time. Presenters may be put on to 'switch *talkback*' where they will hear only what the director wants them to hear.

Opt out
Where regions put their own programmes out over a predetermined period before *opting in* to network, or taking London output.

Out cue
The final sound or vision of a programme, commercial, *promo* or live link. Essential knowledge for whoever is responsible for the next item! A term you may come across on news scripts is SOC – this means Standard Out Cue, the words chosen for the end of every bulletin on that particular station. E.g. 'Peter Baker, GMTV News, Bridgwater.'

Outro
The last few seconds of a programme. It's essential to know how something ends, so you know what to say or when to say it.

PA
The Production Assistant. Co-ordinates virtually all aspects of a television programme and provides a specialist secretarial service; works under the producer and director.

Pan
(In sound:) Shifting a mono sound between left and right.
(In TV:) A horizontal turning of the camera, as in 'pan left'. Vertical movements are called 'tilt' as in 'tilt up'.

P as B
Programme as Broadcast. A highly detailed list produced after a television programme is transmitted. It includes details of crew, library material or stills used, how much contributors or locations were paid, and all the PRS logging details of music used. The P as B is usually done by the *PA* and is essential for speedy and fair payment to everybody. If a programme is all recorded with no live element to be added on transmission, a 'P as C' or Programme as Completed sheet may be written.

Patchbay
See *Jackfield*.

Pedestal
A studio camera mount.

Phantom power
A method of sending microphone or camera power along the same cable that carries the audio or video signal.

Piece to camera
A statement (which may be several sentences) by a presenter or reporter speaking directly to the lens of the camera.

Pilot programme
A one-off trial programme to test its suitability and viability before committing to a series.

Planning (or Facilities)
Most TV stations have a planning department which has to be consulted if you want to book a studio, edit/dubbing suite or preview facility for your programme. You will probably need to give your programme's reference numbers, so the hire charges can be taken off the internal budget.

Popping
The horrible explosion of sound when a speaker is too close to a microphone. 'B' and 'P' sounds are the worst. Pop filters or windshields placed over the microphone may help, but there is no substitute for mouth control and correct microphone placement.

POV
Point of View. A shot from the 'point of view' of whatever you are filming. Say you film a horse galloping along a field, then the horse's point of view would be shot with the camera operator in the saddle.

PPM
Peak Programme Meter. An accurate professional sound meter, which shows true audio peaks, unlike the domestic *VU* (Volume Unit) *Meter*.

Prefade
A switch which lets you hear a sound source before its fader is put up on the sound mixer. Radio presenters have to prefade records, CDs and tapes so they can cue them up. Sometimes called prehear, PFL (prefade listen) or even Piffle!

Presentation
The department in a television station which provides the continuity links and *promos* as well as being responsible for the smooth continuity of output.

Presfax
An internal BBC Teletext system which sends programme and junction information from London to all the regions. Essential knowledge so the regions can *opt out* and in cleanly.

Preview monitor
The vision equivalent of *prefade*. A screen which shows the output of a preselected source, so you can check it before putting it on-air.

Print through
Where the magnetic field on one section of tape affects another when it is wound onto the reel. Particularly noticeable on audio recordings where a very loud passage comes after a very soft one: you hear 'shadows' of loud passage before it actually appears. Temperature and length of storage can affect the amount of print through.

Producer
The person who has total responsibility over a programme or series. In charge of finance and organisation as well as the editorial content, the Producer is essentially the hire-and-fire person.

Programming
The department of a TV or radio station which is concerned with the making of programmes (as opposed to 'Sales' which sells airtime, 'Accounts' which deals with finance, etc.).

Promo
Short for promotion. Also called a trail, this is a short advertisement for a future programme. In both radio and TV, promos are ideal for padding the schedule or programme when there is a timing shortfall, and for dropping when you are overrunning. 'Paid-for-promos', normally tied in with sponsored shows, are treated in the same way as commercials and must never be dropped.

PSC
Portable Single Camera. Used in the same way as *ENG*, it describes a lightweight-camera crew.

Quad
The obsolete system of video tape recording on two-inch-wide tape, using four video heads. If you need to use archive material on this medium, you will have to get it transferred.

Quantel
A trade name for a range of electronic picture processors.

Quarter inch
Tape used for *analogue* reel-to-reel audio recording. Broadcasts speeds are 7 inches per second (ips) and 15 ips on the full width of the tape in one direction.

Radio microphone
Invaluable for TV location work. The presenter has a tiny transmitter in the back pocket while the sound person has the receiver. It's used to record the presenter's voice when he or she is too far away from the sound person's fixed microphone.

Recce
A survey of a location before the shoot to meet interviewees, view prospective camera positions and determine equipment needed.

Redhead
A small television light used on location, usually under 1kW, so called because the main manufacturer paints them red. See *Blonde*.

Red light
Outside a radio or television studio, it means 'do not enter unless it is a dire emergency'. It means that microphones/cameras are 'live' or that a recording is taking place. In a television *gallery* it is especially important to turn red lights on because the switch usually also kills the *colour bar* generators which can bleed through to dark pictures.

Reflector
A large silver or white board or sprung circular hoop which reflects light on to a subject. Used particularly on sunny days to reflect back some sunlight on the side of the face which is in shadow.

Repeat fee
Money paid to presenters, actors or voice-overs, based on an agreed proportion of the original performance fee, when a programme is broadcast for a second time.

Researcher
The person who, working under the producer, finds out facts and contacts, etc. He or she may devise treatments, write scripts and, particularly in ITV, direct items too.

Reverberation
Not 'echo', which is simply a straight reflection of sound rebounding off a surface, or the repeating effect of 'tape echo' which you get when putting the fader up slightly on the tape-recorder which is recording. True reverberation is a complex montage of echoes giving a 'lost in a cave' effect. Widely used in commercial and music production studios.

Reversal film
Film (usually 16 mm) which when processed gives positive pictures like

slide film, and is ready for transmission. Not such good quality or as flexible as negative film, but fine for quick turnaround news and current affairs.

Reverses
The interviewer's in-vision questions filmed after the interview when only one camera is taken onto location. They can be done after the interviewee has left as long as the *eyeline* is reversed.

Ringmain
An internal sound and/or vision distribution system for use within a building.

RJ
Regional journalist. The main newspeople working in a regional TV newsroom.

Rostrum camera
A camera which points down at a programmable moving table to film graphics, photos, newscuttings, etc.

ROT
Recording of Transmission. A tape of exactly what goes on air, not necessarily the same as a 'clean feed' from the studio.

RS
Regionally safe. A BBC continuity term meaning that the network announcer will not mention London's local programmes in the continuity junctions. If they were to mention these, the regions would have to *opt out* and cover these junctions, to talk about their own region's programmes.

Rumble
Unwanted low-frequency turntable noise which can be filtered out on the control desk, usually by a 50 Hz cut button. In other words, every sound under 50 Hz is cut by a certain amount. Every sound over this frequency is unaffected.

Running time
The duration of the programme.

Rushes
Film or video cassettes before being edited. Sometimes called 'road cassettes' or 'original cassettes'.

RV
Rendezvous. A meeting place for location filming detailed on a *call sheet* or *shooting schedule.*

Ryley
A trade name for a caption generator found in the television *gallery* and post-production facilities.

SA
Station Assistant. A general production person, encompassing research, simple graphic and equipment. In BBC TV regions, sometimes called RSA or Regional Station Assistant.

Scanner
Television outside broadcast (*OB*) control van.

Scene dock
The area usually adjacent to the television studio where scenery and props are stored.

Segue
(Pronounced: segway.) Two or more records played 'back to back' on a radio programme with no live link from the presenter.

Selector
A trade name for one of the most widespread computer programmes used to determine radio stations' music running orders.

SEPMAG
Film where the sound is recorded onto quarter-inch tape on location which is transferred onto a separate magnetic spool of 'film' which makes for more flexible and creative editing.

SEPOPT
Film where the sound is recorded onto a separate optical spool of 'film'.

Set
A place in a studio where action is shot.

Sex changer
An adapter used to join together two male or two female plugs.

SFX
Sound effects.

Shooting schedule
A detailed listing of personnel, filming locations, times and outlines of shots required.

Shot list
A list of all the shots filmed on location, logged by the production assistant (*PA*) or *researcher* along with *footage* (film) or *timecode* (video).

Signal-to-noise ratio (SNR)
The ratio of the level of signal to that of the noise of the system. An audio recording peaking 1–2 on the *PPM* will have a low SNR and may sound 'hissy'.

Slate
Film term for the *clapperboard* with all its information on: title, scene and take number. Can be used as a verb as in 'slate it' which means, 'Please can you film the correctly marked-up clapperboard?'

Slide scanner
A machine which turns 35 mm slides into electronic pictures. Sometimes called a telejector or TJ.

SOC
See *Out cue*.

SOF
Literally 'Sound on Film'. Used as a general term for a filmed or video-taped report with sound, as opposed to 'mute'. Not widely used now.

SOPSC, SOENG
'Sound on *PSC*' (or *ENG*) video. Commonly found on news scripts, it means spoken words on a report. Say there are 21 seconds of *actuality* before the interviewee speaks. In other words, the presenter has 21 seconds to voice-over before the words come up. The script will say 'SOPSC @ 21" ____/'. If a *PSC* or *ENG* story is transferred to *VT* it is called SOVT.

SPJ
Senior Production Journalist. A BBC Newsroom term.

Splice
Where two piece of film are joined together. Audio tape joins are normally called 'edits'.

Spun
Fibreglass material clipped over TV lights to diffuse them.

Squark box
Slang name for open microphone intercom system. Usually found between studios, galleries, newsrooms and production offices.

Standards converter
A machine which converts one system of video signal into another. For example, video programmes made using the America NTSC system have to be put through a standards converter so that they can be seen on the UK's PAL system.

Stedicam
Trade name for patented gyroscopic harness system which keeps a camera very steady.

Steenbeck
A trade name for the sturdy film-editing tables used throughout broadcasting.

Still store
A digital storage device used to keep a number of stills. Sometimes written as 'SS'.

Storyboard
Rough cartoon depiction of each shot, to give everybody concerned an idea of how the finished scene or film will look.

Strand
A regular feature in a topical programme.

Super
To superimpose one image over another. 'Super Cap' written on a script would mean 'superimpose the caption'.

Switching (or COMMS or Central Transmission Facilities)
The department in a television station through which audio and visual signals are monitored and connected; both in and out of the station.

Syndication
An arrangement by which duplicated programmes may be sent on tape or relayed to a number of different radio or television stations. A financial and licensing arrangement.

TA
Technical Assistant. (See *BA*.)

Tag
A differing *outro* line of a promotion or commercial. For example, a twenty-second radio commercial may have the same first seventeen seconds in all versions, but have different versions with different tags. For example, 'open tomorrow till eight'; 'closed tomorrow but open Monday', etc.

Tail out
Winding audio or video tape backwards so its end ('tail') is pointing out to the world. storing tape this way is said to prevent *print through*.

Talkback
A sound link between the studio and the gallery. Television presenters may be on switch talkback where they hear only what the *gallery* want them to hear or open talkback where the communication with the gallery is uninterrupted

Tarif
(Technical Apparatus for the Rectification of Indifferent Film). A verb, meaning to alter the brightness, contrast or colour of a picture signal. Usually done by vision engineers in the *gallery*. Journalists are forever asking vision engineers to make some old faded colour slide they have found for their story look better by 'tarifing' it.

TC
The BBC's internal abbreviation for Television Centre. The complex at Wood Lane in London is based around a huge, purpose-built circular structure know to architecture fans as the 'concrete doughnut'.

Tease
A brief mention, usually before a radio commercial break, of an item or song which is coming up.

Telecine
A machine which converts moving film into television pictures. Also known as TK and not TC partly for historical reasons and partly because the BBC's Television Centre in London is known as TC.

Timecode
An electronic counter encoded onto video tape which is never broadcast. It makes finding shots, editing and synchronisation simple. The numbers mean hours (or tape numbers); minutes; seconds; frames.

TM
Technical Manager. The person in charge of the technical quality of all the studio operations.

TO
Technical Operator. A fairly junior programming/technical position in a radio station. This person operates the on-air desk during taped or fed-in programmes, and may record news feeds as well as a host of other activities.

Tone
An electronically generated noise, usually a sine wave of 1kHz used to *line up* audio equipment, or the audio sections of video gear.

Trail (er)
A short promotional item advertising a future programme.

Transfer
To rerecord from one system to another, say film to videotape, or DAT onto quarter-inch tape.

Two shot
A shot with two people in it.

Uher
Portable reel-to-reel tape-recorders using five-inch-diameter spools, very robust but very heavy and expensive to maintain. More people are using the lighter and cheaper portable cassette machines like the *Marantz*, or one of the many *DAT* recorders, even though you have to usually transfer the sound from the cassette in order to edit.

U-Matic
The Sony video recording system using three-quarter-inch tape in chunky cassettes. There are two semi-compatible electronic formats using the same tapes, Low Band and the better quality High Band.

Under run
Where a programme falls short of its planned duration and everyone panics.

Understudy
An actor who can replace another at short notice. Presenters who do this are usually called 'fill-ins'.

Unit Manager
May also be known as production manager. The person mainly

responsible for personnel, budgeting and resourcing television programmes, and is not usually involved in studio or location work.

Vents

The air conditioning in a studio which is usually automatically switched
off when a microphone is switched on, or else the *compressors* in the
sound circuits will bring up the vent noise in the silent gaps to sound like
a howling gale!

VHS

Video Home System. The domestic cassette system used by professionals to edit programmes '*off line*'. The (incompatible) superior system
is Super VHS or S-VHS.

Vision mixer

Used to describe both the operator and the mixing panel they operate.

VO

Voice-over. Some broadcasters write on scripts: OOV (Out of Vision) or
COMM (commentary). This can be a section of a programme where an
in-vision presenter is temporarily out of vision, or it can describe the
voice of a person who is never in-vision.

Vox pop

'Vox populi' translated from Latin means 'voice of the people' – asking
the public their views on various topics.

VT

Video tape.

VT clock

An electronically generated clock used to identify the programme and
giving an exact countdown to its start. It cuts to black at minus three seconds in case it is accidentally cut to air.

VTR

Video tape-recorder.

VU Meter

A meter used to measure sound volume units. A *PPM* or peak programme meter is much more accurate for broadcasting work.

WA

Wide angle. The lens or attachment put onto the camera to create the
effect. Sometimes affectionately known as 'the wangle'.

Walk-on
See *Extra*.

Whip pan
To *pan* violently as was famously used in between scenes of *The Man from UNCLE* programmes.

White balance
Where an electronic camera is adjusted so that the colours will register correctly, even in yellower, artificial light conditions. Normally a piece of white card is placed in front of the lens and the white balance button is pushed on the camera, and the camera automatically compensates.

Wildtrack
Background atmosphere recording which may be used in the final edited film to disguise any mismatched sound. Also known as *buzz track*.

Wipe
A transition between two pictures using a moving edge, in a variety of different shapes and angles. A fairly dated effect now that *DVEs* are in use everywhere and many domestic video mixers have a wipe facility.

Wobblevision
Slang for poor, hand-held camera work.

Wrap (as in 'It's a wrap.')
Wind, reel and print. The old movie term for 'We've finished filming, time to go home for tea.'

WS
Wide shot. Includes the whole set or most of it.

X
Crosses. On a TV or stage script you may see XU (crosses upstage) and XD (crosses downstage), etc.

Zoom
A lens with variable angle of view.

TV script jargon

It would be impossible for me to list a definitive glossary of terms you'll find on TV scripts, because they vary from station to station and even different programmes have their own methods of saying the same thing.

For example: **OOV = VO = COMM.** All mean an
OUT OF VISION
VOICE-OVER doing a
COMMENTARY

Another audio term: **UP ¼″** is the same as **ROLL TAPE** and means that sound is being played in on ¼″ audio tape.

You will soon get used to all the abbreviations and jargon, but don't be afraid to ask the floor manager or director if you're unsure of anything.

Terms marked with an asterisk * are explained in greater detail in the A–Z directory on the previous pages.

ANIMATE	Changing a graphic so words or pictures appear.
ASTON SUPER	A caption superimposed (Aston is the tradename of a caption generator).
CAM CAP	Camera caption, literally a piece of card in front of a camera.
CLIP	Short extract of another programme or film.
COMM	Commentary.*
CRAWLER	Caption that 'crawls' along width of screen.
CSO*	Chromatic Separation Overlay (usually BBC) or Chromakey (ITV).
CU	Close-up.
CUT	An instantaneous transition from one shot to another.
DUR	Duration.
DVE*	Digital Video Effect.
FX	Effects. (SFX=Sound effects.)
GRAMS*	'Gramophone' meaning off disc.
GV*	General view.
IN VIS	In vision.
MIX	A dissolve from one shot to another.
OOV	Out of vision.
PTC	Piece to camera.*
Q DOT	Cue dot,* which tells transmission staff when to run breaks.
RT	Running time.*

RX — Recording date/time.
SEPMAG* — Separate magnetic film and sound.
SOF* — Sound on film.
SOT — Sound on tape.
SOVT — Sound on video tape.
STRAP — A caption along a horizontal band on the screen.
STING — Musical piece.
TC* — Television Centre (BBC).
TJ — 35 mm slide (lit: Telejector, the old slide scanner* machine).
TK — Telecine*.
TKKR — Telecine keeps running.
TX — Transmission date/time.
UP — As in UP VT, meaning the video tape appears on screen.
VT — Video tape.
WIPE* — A transition from one shot to another using a moving edge.
WS* — Wide shot.

Piatkus Business Books

Piatkus Business and Career guides have been created for people who need expert knowledge readily available in a clear and easy-to-follow format. Written by specialists in their field these books will help you improve your skills and develop your career path so that you can achieve your professional and personal goals. Titles include:

Careers

The 10-Day MBA: A step-by-step guide to mastering the skills taught in top business schools Steven Silbiger

10 Steps To The Top: How to climb your own mountain and achieve your potential Marie Jennings

How To Find The Perfect Job: A step-by-step guide Tom Jackson

The Influential Woman: How to achieve success in your career – and still enjoy your personal life Lee Bryce

Marketing Yourself: How to sell yourself and get the jobs you've always wanted Dorothy Leeds

Networking And Mentoring: A woman's guide Dr Lily M. Segerman-Peck

The Perfect CV: How to get the job you really want Tom
  Jackson

**Perfect Job Search Strategies: More than 100 proven
  strategies for getting the job you want in today's challenging market** Tom Jackson

Presenting Yourself: A personal image guide for men
  Mary Spillane

Presenting Yourself: A personal image guide for women
  Mary Spillane

**Secrets Of Successful Interviews: Tactics and strategies
  for winning the job you really want** Dorothy Leeds

**Which Way Now? How to plan and develop a successful
  career** Bridget Wright

Public Speaking and Presentation

**Confident Conversation: How to talk in any business or
  social situation** Dr Lillian Glass

**Confident Speaking: How to communicate effectively
  using the Power Talk System** Christian H. Godefroy and
  Stephanie Barrat

**Powerspeak: The complete guide to public speaking and
  presentation** Dorothy Leeds

Say What You Mean And Get What You Want George R.
  Walther

Personal Development

**10-Minute Time And Stress Management: How to gain
  an extra 10 hours a week** Dr David Lewis

Brain Power: The 12-week mental training programme
  Marilyn vos Savant and Leonore Fleischer

**The Complete Book Of Business Etiquette: The essential
  guide to getting ahead in business** Lynne Brennan and
  David Block

**Creative Thinking: How to generate ideas and turn them
  into successful reality** Michael LeBoeuf

Getting What You Want: Power persuasion techniques to use at home and at work Quentin de la Bedoyere

He Says, She Says: Closing the communication gap between the sexes Dr Lillian Glass

How To Develop And Profit From Your Creative Powers Michael LeBoeuf

How To Survive Without A Job: Practical solutions for developing skills and building self-esteem Ursula Markham

Memory Booster: Easy techniques for rapid learning and a better memory Robert W. Finkel

Mind Power: Use positive thinking to change your life Christian H. Godefroy with D. R. Steevens

Napoleon Hill's Keys To Success Matthew Sartwell (editor)

Napoleon Hill's Unlimited Success: 52 steps to personal and financial reward Matthew Sartwell (editor)

NLP: The new art and science of getting what you want Dr Harry Alder

Personal Power: How to achieve influence and success in your professional life Philippa Davies

Play To Your Strengths: Focus on what you do best – and success will follow Donald O. Clifton and Paula Nelson

Quantum Learning: Unleash the genius within you Bobbi DePorter with Mike Hernacki

Total Confidence: The complete guide to self-assurance and personal success Philippa Davies

Working For Yourself: How to have a successful career Roz Morris

Your Total Image: How to communicate success Philippa Davies

Writing and Journalism

1000 Markets For Freelance Writers: An A–Z guide to general and specialist magazines and journals Robert Palmer

How To Make Money From Freelance Writing Andrew
  Crofts
Interviewing For Journalists Joan Clayton
Journalism For Beginners Joan Clayton